MS-Excel 97 explained

by

N. Kantaris
and
P.R.M. Oliver

GW00729028

BERNARD BABANI (publishing) LTD.
THE GRAMPIANS
SHEPHERDS BUSH ROAD
LONDON W6 7NF
ENGLAND

PLEASE NOTE

Although every care has been taken with the production of this book to ensure that any projects, designs, modifications and/or programs, etc., contained herewith, operate in a correct and safe manner and also that any components specified are normally available in Great Britain, the Publishers and Author(s) do not accept responsibility in any way for the failure (including fault in design) of any project, design, modification or program to work correctly or to cause damage to any equipment that it may be connected to or used in conjunction with, or in respect of any other damage or injury that may be so caused, nor do the Publishers accept responsibility in any way for the failure to obtain specified components.

Notice is also given that if equipment that is still under warranty is modified in any way or used or connected with home-built equipment then that warranty may be void

© 1997 BERNARD BABANI (publishing) LTD

First Published – September 1997
Reprinted – November 1998

British Library Cataloguing in Publication Data:
A catalogue record for this book is available from the British Library

ISBN 0 85934 429 0

Cover Design by Gregor Arthur
Cover illustration by Adam Willis
Printed and bound in Great Britain by Cox & Wyman Ltd, Reading

ABOUT THIS BOOK

MS-Excel 97 explained has been written for those who want to get to grips with the latest 3-dimensional spreadsheet for Windows 95 from Microsoft, in the fastest possible time. The material in this book is presented on the 'what you need to know first, appears first' basis, although the underlying structure is such that slightly more experienced users need not start at the beginning and go right through to the end; they can start from any section, as each section of the book has been designed to be self contained.

No previous knowledge of spreadsheets is assumed, so that users without any knowledge of the subject can follow the book easily, but we do not describe how to set up your computer hardware, or how to install and use Windows 95. If you need to know more about the Windows environment, then may we suggest you select an appropriate level book for your needs from the 'Books Available' list - the books are graduated in complexity with the less demanding *One step at a time* series, to the more detailed *Explained* series. They are all published by BERNARD BABANI (publishing) Ltd.

Microsoft Excel 97 is a very powerful spreadsheet package that has the ability to work 3-dimensionally with both multiple worksheets and files. It is operated by selecting commands from drop-down menus, by using buttons, or by writing 'macros' to chain together menu commands. Each method of accessing the package is discussed separately, but the emphasis is mostly in the area of menu-driven and button clicking command selection. Working under the Windows 95 environment, gives the package an excellent WYSIWYG (What You See Is What You Get) appearance which, in turn, allows for the production of highly professional quality printed material.

Most features of the package will be discussed using simple examples that the user is encouraged to type in, save, and modify as more advanced features are introduced. This provides the new user with a set of examples that aim to help with the learning process, and should help to provide the confidence needed to tackle some of the more advanced capabilities of the package later.

For those who would like to practise with additional examples, slightly unguided, but with enough instruction so that they can be completed successfully, we have included three exercises in the penultimate chapter of the book. The exercises are drawn from sufficiently general topics, so as to maximise their suitability to your needs and understanding.

Although the book is intended as a supplement to the 'Help' documentation that comes with the package, in the last chapter of the book, all the Excel 97 functions are listed so that it is self contained and can be used as a reference long after you become an expert in the use of the program.

ABOUT THE AUTHORS

Noel Kantaris graduated in Electrical Engineering at Bristol University and after spending three years in the Electronics Industry in London, took up a Tutorship in Physics at the University of Queensland. Research interests in Ionospheric Physics, led to the degrees of M.E. in Electronics and Ph.D. in Physics. On return to the UK, he took up a Post-Doctoral Research Fellowship in Radio Physics at the University of Leicester, and then in 1973 a lecturing position in Engineering at the Camborne School of Mines, Cornwall, (part of Exeter University), where since 1978 he has also assumed the responsibility for the Computing Department.

Phil Oliver graduated in Mining Engineering at Camborne School of Mines in 1967 and since then has specialised in most aspects of surface mining technology, with a particular emphasis on computer related techniques. He has worked in Guyana, Canada, several Middle Eastern countries, South Africa and the United Kingdom, on such diverse projects as: the planning and management of bauxite, iron, gold and coal mines; rock excavation contracting in the UK; international mining equipment sales and technical back up and international mine consulting for a major mining house in South Africa. In 1988 he took up a lecturing position at Camborne School of Mines (part of Exeter University) in Surface Mining and Management.

ACKNOWLEDGEMENTS

We would like to thank the staff of Text 100 Limited for providing the software programs on which this work was based. We would also like to thank colleagues at the Camborne School of Mines for the helpful tips and suggestions which assisted us in the writing of this book.

TRADEMARKS

Arial and **Times New Roman** are registered trademarks of The Monotype Corporation plc.

HP and LaserJet are registered trademarks of Hewlett Packard Corporation.

IBM is a registered trademark of International Business Machines, Inc.

Intel is a registered trademark of Intel Corporation.

Lotus, 1-2-3 is a registered trademark of Lotus Development Corporation.

Microsoft, **MS-DOS**, **Windows**, **Windows NT**, **Works**, and **Visual Basic**, are either registered trademarks or trademarks of Microsoft Corporation.

PostScript is a registered trademark of Adobe Systems Incorporated.

TrueType is a registered trademark of Apple Corporation.

All other brand and product names used in the book are recognised as trademarks, or registered trademarks, of their respective companies.

CONTENTS

1. PACKAGE OVERVIEW

Microsoft Excel 97 is a powerful and versatile software package which has proved its usefulness, not only in the business world, but also within the scientific and engineering spheres. The program's power lies in its ability to emulate everything that can be done by the use of pencil, paper and a calculator. It is an 'electronic spreadsheet' or simply a 'spreadsheet', and its power is derived from the power of the computer it is running on, and the flexibility and accuracy with which it can deal with the solution of the various applications it is programmed to manage. These can vary from budgeting and forecasting to the solution of complex scientific and engineering problems.

Microsoft Excel 97 for Windows 95 is backwards compatible to spreadsheets built up on previous versions of Excel or, indeed, to other spreadsheets, such as Lotus 1-2-3, Quattro Pro, and Microsoft Works, which can easily be made to run on this version of Excel. Once you have overcome the first hurdle and started to use Excel 97, you will find it both intuitive and an easy program to produce the type of work output you would not have dreamt possible.

Excel, in common with all other MS Office 97 applications, makes use of IntelliSense, which anticipates what you want to do and produces the correct result. For example, AutoCorrect and Auto-Format can, when activated, correct common spelling mistakes and format an entire workbook automatically. Other Wizards can help you with everyday tasks and/or make complex tasks easier to manage.

With OfficeLinks and OLE (Object Linking and Embedding), you can move and share information seamlessly between MS Office 97 applications by simply dragging information from one application to another. Finally, Microsoft Visual Basic for Applications, gives you a powerful and flexible development platform for creating custom solutions.

Hardware Requirements

If Microsoft Excel 97 is already installed on your computer, you can safely skip this and the next two sections of this chapter.

To install and run Excel 97 successfully, you need an IBM compatible PC equipped with Intel's 80486 (or higher) processor. We recommend a minimum processor speed of 66MHz. In addition, you need the following:

- Windows 95, Windows NT or Windows NT Advanced Server version.

- Random access memory (RAM): 8MB; 16MB recommended when running Excel workbooks.

- Hard disc space available for MS-Excel 97: 31.2MB for Excel and 10MB for converters, filters, and data access tools.

- Video adapter: VGA or higher resolution. If you are embedding colour pictures, you will need a 256-colour video adapter.

- Pointing device: Microsoft Mouse or compatible.

Realistically, to run Microsoft Excel 97 with reasonably sized workbooks, you will need a Pentium PC with at least 16MB of RAM. To run Microsoft Excel 97 from a network, you must also have a network compatible with your Windows operating environment, such as Microsoft's Windows 95, Windows NT, LAN Manager, or Novell's NetWare.

Although it is possible to operate from the keyboard alone, the availability of a mouse is a must if you are going to benefit from the program's features. After all, pointing and clicking at an option on the screen, is a lot easier than having to learn several different key combinations.

Major Excel Features

Some of the major features Microsoft Excel 97 contains, include the ability to:

- Enter and edit data directly in a cell or in the formula bar, and to check your spelling.

- Manage data simply by treating all files as workbooks.

- Use the Find File command to search for a workbook, even if its name is not known.

- Use the Format Painter button to quickly copy formats between cells and between objects.

- Create named ranges in the Name box on the formula bar.

- Create custom AutoFill series and automatically create grand totals with AutoSum.

- Use the AutoCalculate facility which produces the sum of a selected range automatically and displays it on the Status bar at the bottom of the screen.

- Use the AutoComplete facility which allows you to type the first few letters of an entry in a cell, then use the right-mouse button to complete the entry from a list, based on the entries you have already made in that column.

- Use the AutoCorrect facility which when selected, can correct common mistakes as you type.

- Create 3-D formulae and 3-D names for powerful workbook models.

- Drag data directly onto a chart to add a data series or data points, and add trendlines and error bars to your data series.

- Use the improved drag-and-drop editing facility which can be used to easily move or copy selected ranges between worksheets and workbooks.

- Draw graphic objects directly on charts and to position objects, such as titles, anywhere you want them.

- Sort data by using column labels from a list and the creation of custom sort orders, such as High, Med, and Low.

- Access external databases with Microsoft Query and the use of the interactive PivotTable facility to cross-tabulate and summarise data from an existing list or table.

- Use the Scenario Manager to create, manage, and track changes to scenarios.

- Use or customise any of the built-in toolbars, or create your own.

- Use autotemplates to create new default workbooks and sheets.

- Use the Visual Basic Programming language to create custom solutions in Microsoft Excel.

- Display the precedent, dependent, and error tracers directly on your worksheet to locate problems in formulae.

- Use the Object Linking and Embedding (OLE) facility to link objects without leaving Microsoft Excel.

- Solve What-if problems by seeking a value that solves a formula.

- Use the Solver to analyse multiple-variable problems.

- Use the Data Analysis Tool to make statistical or engineering analysis easier.

- Add explanatory information, called cell tips, to individual worksheet cells.

- Analyse sales or market research data by geographical regions by arranging your data in columns on a worksheet.

- Find, open, or manage documents in the same way as in all the other MS-Office applications.

- Create shared lists so that several users can work with the same data.

Other features deal with formatting numbers, charts, organising data, and retrieving and analysing data from lists and tables.

New Features in Excel 97:

Some of the major enhancements Microsoft Excel 97 has over previous releases of the package allow you to:

- Use multiple Undo - for up to the last 16 actions.

- Use the 'Yes to All' option when closing multiple files

- Use the IntelliMouse pointing device - a new mouse introduced with the release of Office 97. You can use the wheel button of this new mouse to scroll or zoom your view of a worksheet and drill up and down on data in PivotTables, outlines, and subtotalled lists.

- Easily locate the row and column headings that apply to the active cell - as you highlight a cell, the row number and column letter 'light up'.

- Share the new drawing tools with other Office 97 applications.

- Use the new Graphics Interchange Format (.gif) and JPEG File Interchange Format (.jpg) filters to export charts in common graphics formats so they can be displayed on the World Wide Web.

- Use up to 32,000 characters in a cell, increased from 255.

- Use up to 65,536 rows per worksheet, increased from 16,384.

- Use Queries which now run in the background, so that you can continue to work in Excel while data is being retrieved.

- Recommend worksheet functions by typing a brief description of what you want to do. The Office Assistant then suggests which worksheet functions to use.

- Use row and column labels in formulae to refer to cells without using cell references or creating names.

- Rotate text in cells to any angle, which lets you produce vertical labels.

- Use the new Chart Wizard, which is integrated with the tabbed dialogue boxes and options, to format and edit your charts.

- Add menus to toolbars or toolbar buttons to menus. The image associated with a menu command shows you what the command will look like if you choose to display it as a button.

Obviously, the list of enhancements does not end here.

Most features of the package (old and new) will be discussed using simple examples that the user is encouraged to type in, save, and modify as more advanced features are introduced. This provides the new user with a set of examples that aim to help with the learning of the most commonly used features of the package, and should help to provide the confidence needed to tackle some of the more advanced features of the package later.

Installing Excel 97

Installing Excel 97 on your computer's hard disc is made very easy with the use of the SETUP program, which even configures Excel automatically to take advantage of the computer's hardware.

If you are installing from floppy discs, insert the first SETUP disc (Disc 1) in the A: drive, or if you are installing from a CD-ROM, insert the CD in the CD-ROM drive. If you are installing from a network drive, make a note of the drive letter because you will need it later. Then do the following:

* Click the **Start** button on the Windows 95 Taskbar and select **Settings, Control Panel**.

* On the displayed Control Panel window, double-click the Add/Remove Programs icon, shown here.

* On the Add/Remove Programs Properties dialogue box, click the Install/Uninstall tab and press the **Install** button.

* SETUP will scan your disc for already installed parts of Microsoft Office and will advise you as to the folder in which you should install Excel. This will most likely be **Msoffice**.

* Follow the SETUP instructions on the screen, until the installation of Microsoft Excel program files is complete.

The SETUP program will modify your system files automatically and will create a new entry in the **Start, Programs** cascade menu, with the icon shown here. Clicking this menu entry will start Microsoft Excel.

If you have MS-Office 97 installed, SETUP also adds Excel to the Microsoft Shortcut Bar facility (see next page).

The Office Shortcut Bar:

During installation, the Office Shortcut Bar is collated and added to the Windows Start Up program so that it will be displayed automatically on your screen whenever you start your PC. The contents of a Microsoft Shortcut Bar used with a previous version of Office will be preserved. The Shortcut Bar will be displayed when you restart your computer.

The Microsoft Office Shortcut Bar, provides a convenient way to work with your documents and the Office applications by complementing the Windows **Start** menu.

The various icons on the Shortcut Bar, shown here, have the following functions:

Getting Results Book

New Office Document

Open Office Document

Microsoft Bookshelf Basics

New Note

New Message

New Journal Entry

Microsoft Outlook

New Appointment

New Task

New Contact

The first icon of the above Office Toolbar (Getting Results Book) is only available to you if you are connected to a company's network or the Internet and have installed a browser, such as Microsoft's Explorer, or Netscape. This option allows you to use browser-style query techniques on both HTML and Office documents on an internal network or the Internet.

The function of other icons on the toolbar is as follows:

The New Office Document button: Allows you to select in the displayed dialogue box the tab containing the type of document you want to work with. Double-clicking the type of document or template you want, automatically loads the appropriate application.

The Open Office Document button: Allows you to work with an existing document. Opening a document, first starts the application originally used to create it.

The Microsoft Bookshelf Basics: Allows a preview of the world of information found in the complete version of the Bookshelf which provides access to three major reference books; _The American Heritage Dictionary_, _The Original Roget's Thesaurus_, and _The Columbia Dictionary of Quotations_. This facility requires you to have the CD-ROM.

The New buttons: Allows you to make a New Note, a New Message, or a New Journal Entry to schedule your time effectively.

The Microsoft Outlook button: Activates the Office 97 new desktop manager used to manage your e-mail, contact lists, tasks and documents.

The New Appointment button: Allows you to add a new appointment in your management system. This caters for all-day or multiple-day events and a meeting planner, including meeting request processing and attendance lists.

The New Task button: Allows you to add a new task in your management system, including automatic composition of an e-mail message summarising a task and automatic tracking of tasks sent to other users.

The New Contact button: Allows you to enter a new contact in Outlook's database, or to send an e-mail message direct from the contact manager and use hyperlinks for direct access to a contact's home page on the Internet.

The Mouse Pointers

In Microsoft Excel 97, as with all other graphical based programs, the use of a mouse makes many operations both easier and more fun to carry out.

Excel makes use of the mouse pointers available in Windows 95, some of the most common of which are illustrated below. When Excel is initially started up the first you will see is the hourglass, which turns into either an upward pointing hollow arrow or a hollow cross, depending on the area you point to. Other shapes depend on the type of work you are doing at the time.

The hourglass which displays when you are waiting while performing a function.

The arrow which appears when the pointer is placed over menus, toolbars, scrolling bars, and buttons.

The hollow cross which appears when the pointer is placed within the worksheet area.

The I-beam which appears when editing a cell or in text areas of the screen.

The large 4-headed arrow which appears after choosing the **Control, Move/Size** command(s) for moving or sizing windows.

The double arrows which appear when over the border of a window, used to drag the side and alter the size of the window.

The Help hand which appears in the Help windows, and is used to access 'hypertext' type links.

Excel, like other Windows applications, has additional mouse pointers which facilitate the execution of selected commands. The shape of some pointers is mostly self-evident, while others, shown below, have the following functions:

↓   The vertical pointer which appears when pointing over a column in a worksheet and used to select the column.

→   The horizontal pointer which appears when pointing at a row in a worksheet and used to select the row.

←||→   The vertical split arrow which appears when pointing at the vertical split box or over the area separating two columns in a worksheet and used to either split the screen or size a column.

⇅   The horizontal split arrow which appears when pointing at the horizontal split box or over the area separating two rows in a worksheet and used to either split the screen or size the row.

+   The frame cross which you drag to create a frame.

↑   The draw pointer which appears when you are drawing freehand.

Some Excel operations display a '?' button, as shown here. Clicking this button changes the mouse pointer from its usual shape to the 'What's this?' shape. Pointing with this to an object in the dialogue box or window and left-clicking, gives additional information, as we shall see shortly.

11

Using the Office Assistant

The Office Assistant is a central source of application information. No matter which Office 97 application you are using, the Assistant is there to help you.

To find out how it works, click the Office Assistant button, shown here, with the left mouse button, type the word *help* in the displayed 'What would you like to do?' box, shown to the left, and left-click the **Search** button.

A list of help topics is then displayed, as shown to the right. To see more topics, left-click the small triangle at the bottom of the list. To find out how you can use the Office Assistant, click the 'Ways to get assistance while you work' option which causes the display of the screen shown on the next page. From this latter screen you can find out all there is to know about the Office Assistant.

The very same screen can be displayed from all Office applications, with only the title of the window changing to reflect the application in use.

Clicking the left mouse button on areas of the screen that causes the mouse pointer to change to a pointing hand (there are five such areas), displays additional information on the selected topic. The changed pointer is shown at the bottom of the above screen dump.

Customising the Office Assistant:

You can customise the Office Assistant to a great degree. Not only can you change the way it responds to your enquiries, but you can switch it off once you have mastered Excel 97.

To see the default options settings of the Office Assistant, activate it, left-click on it, and left-click the **Options** button on the displayed box, shown here.

Doing this, causes the following dialogue box to be displayed on your screen:

13

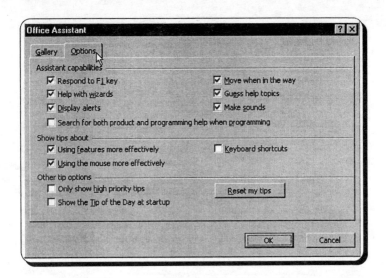

As you can see, it is possible to choose from several options. Should you want to change the shape of your Office Assistant (there are nine shapes to choose from - see next page), either left-click the Gallery tab of the above dialogue box, or right-click the Office Assistant and select the **Choose Assistant** option from the displayed menu, as shown below.

Either action displays the following dialogue box in which you can select your preferred Assistant shape by left-clicking the **Next** button.

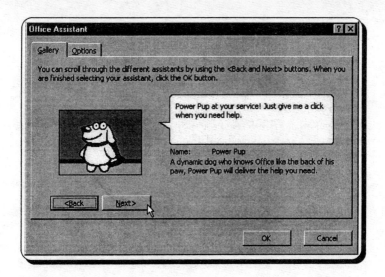

The shapes of the available Assistants are as follows:

Using the Help Menu

Another way of getting help in an Office application is to left-click the **Help** menu option at the top of the application window, and select the **Contents and Index** option of the displayed sub-menu, shown here. This displays the Contents dialogue box, shown below.

You can either view information on the screen or print it on paper. Left-clicking the Find tab, displays a dialogue box with three areas for typing, selecting and displaying information, as shown below.

Typing, for example, the words **_find fast_** in the first 'Find' box, causes a list of related topics to appear automatically in the second 'Select' box. Selection of one or more matching words from the displayed list narrows down the selection of topics appearing in the third 'Display' box.

Finally, selecting a topic from the third display box by left-clicking it to highlight it and pressing the **Display** button at the bottom of the dialogue box, produces information on your selection.

If the topic you want to select is not visible within the display area of the third box, use the scroll bar to get to it.

As an exercise, click the Index tab of the Help Topics dialogue box and type the word 'open' in the first text box. Immediately the topic 'Opening files' appears in the second text box, as shown below.

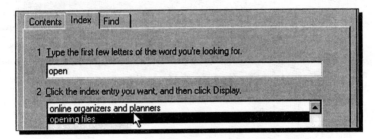

Next, double-click on the selected item to display all you need to know, in this instance, about the Excel 97, 95, and 6.0 file formats. Similar searches carried out from other Office 97 applications will reveal what you should do if you require backward compatibility.

It is worth while exploring the different ways in which you can get help with or without the Office Assistant. For example, you can implement the **F1** function key to give you context sensitive help whenever you press it. To find out how to do this, select the 'Getting help without the Office Assistant' option in the 'What would you like to do?' list (see page 12).

Another way of getting context sensitive help is to select the **'What's This'** option from the **Help** sub-menu, then move the modified mouse pointer to an area of the document, or onto a particular Toolbar button, and press the left mouse button.

2. THE EXCEL SPREADSHEET

Starting the Excel Program

Excel is started in Windows either by clicking the **Start** button then selecting **Program** and clicking on the 'Microsoft Excel' icon on the cascade menu, or by clicking the Excel icon on the Old Office Shortcut Bar, or by clicking the 'Open a Document' icon on the Office Shortcut Bar and double-clicking on an Excel worksheet file. In the latter case the worksheet will be loaded into Excel at the same time.

If you have used a previous version of Excel it might be a good idea to use **The Office Assistant** (see end of previous chapter) and search for *what's new*. Selecting the 'What's New in Microsoft Excel 97?' option (pointed to below), displays a further list of options which you might like to view.

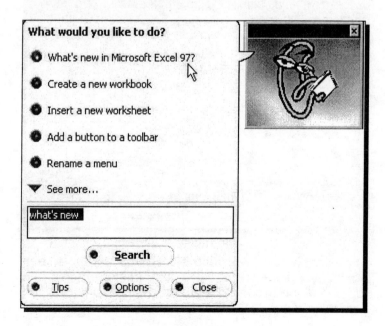

The Excel Screen

When Excel is loaded, a 'blank' spreadsheet screen displays with a similar Title bar, Menu bar, Toolbar and Formatting bar to those of Word. Obviously there are some differences, but that is to be expected as the two programs serve different purposes.

The opening screen of Excel is shown below. It is perhaps worth looking at the various parts that make up this screen, or window, if only to see how similar it is to that of Word. Excel follows the usual Microsoft Windows conventions with which you are probably familiar by now.

The window as shown above takes up the full screen area. If you click on the application restore button, the top one of the two restore buttons at the top right of the screen, you can make Excel show in a smaller window.

This can be useful when you are running several applications at the same time and you want to transfer between them with the mouse.

Note that the Excel window, which in this case displays an empty and untitled book (Book1), has some areas which have identical functions to those of other Microsoft Office applications, and other areas which have different functions. Below, we describe first the areas that are common to other MS-Office applications and then those that are exclusive to Excel.

Area	*Function*
Command Buttons	Clicking on the top command button, (see upper-left corner of the window), displays a pull-down menu which can be used to restore, move, size, maximise, minimise, and close the program window. The lower command button controls the current worksheet window in the same manner.
Title Bar	The bar at the top of a window which displays the application name and the name of the current document.
Minimise Button	Clicking this button minimises a worksheet to an icon, or the application to the Windows Taskbar.
Restore Button	When clicked on, this button restores the active window to the position and size that was occupied before it was

21

maximised. The restore button is then replaced by a Maximise button, as shown here, which is used to set the window to full screen size.

Close Button | The extreme top right button that you click to close a window.

Menu Bar | The bar below the Title bar which allows you to choose from several menu options. Clicking on a menu item displays the pull-down menu associated with that item.

Toolbar | The bar below the Menu bar which contains buttons that give you mouse-click access to the functions most often used in the program. These are grouped according to function.

Formatting Bar | The buttons on the Formatting Bar allow you to change the attributes of a font, such as italic and underline, and also to format text in various ways. The Formatting Bar contains two boxes; a font box and a size box which show which font and size of characters are currently being used. These boxes give access to other installed fonts and character sizes.

Split Box | The area above the top vertical scroll button which when dragged allows you to split the screen.

Scroll Bars	The areas on the screen (extreme right and bottom of each window) that contain scroll boxes in vertical and horizontal bars. Clicking on these bars allows you to control the part of a document which is visible on the screen.
Scroll Arrows	The arrowheads at each end of each scroll bar at which you can click to scroll the screen up and down one line, or left and right 10% of the screen, at a time.
Status Bar	The bottom line of the window that displays status inform-ation, and in which a short help description appears when you point and click on a button.
Edit line	Contains the selection indicator (cell co-ordinates), and the name box that identifies the selected cell, chart item, or drawing object. The edit line box can display a number, a label, or the formula behind a result.
Cell Pointer	Marks the current cell.
Column letter	The letter that identifies each column.
Row number	The number that identifies each row.
Tab buttons	Clicking on these buttons, scrolls sheet tabs right or left, when there are more tabs than can be displayed at once.

Current sheet	Shows the current sheet amongst a number of sheets in a file. These are named Sheet1, Sheet2, Sheet3, and so on, by default, but can be changed to, say, North, South, East, and West. Clicking on a sheet tab, moves you to that sheet.
Tab split box	The split box which you drag left to see more of the scroll bar, or right to see more tabs.

Excel 97 has two split boxes, which are used to split the screen horizontally or vertically. One of these is located at the extreme right of the screen above the 'top vertical scroll arrow' button, and is identified on Excel's worksheet screen dump shown on page 20. The other is located at the extreme bottom-right corner of the screen, to the left of the 'right horizontal scroll arrow' button, but is not identified on our screen dump. Both of these have to do with splitting the screen; the identified one horizontally, the other vertically. The use of both these split boxes will be discussed later.

The Menu Bar Options:

Each menu bar option has associated with it a pull-down sub-menu. To activate the menu, either press the <Alt> key, which causes the first option of the menu (in this case the current Book Control Menu box) to be highlighted, then use the right and left arrow keys to highlight any of the options in the menu, or use the mouse to point to an option. Pressing either the <Enter> key, or the left mouse button, reveals the pull-down sub-menu of the highlighted menu option.

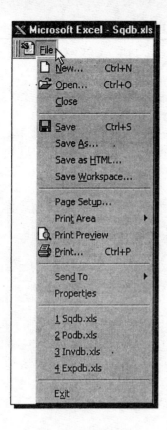

Menu options can also be activated directly by pressing the <Alt> key followed by the underlined letter of the required option. Thus, pressing <Alt+F>, causes the pull-down sub-menu of the **File** menu to be displayed, as shown here. You can use the up and down arrow keys to move the highlighted bar up and down a sub-menu, or the right and left arrow keys to move along the options in the menu bar.

As you move up and down a sub-menu, a brief description of the high-lighted option appears in the Status bar. Pressing the <Enter> key selects the option or executes the option command. Pressing the <Esc> key once, closes the pull-down sub-menu, while pressing it a second time, closes the menu system.

Some sub-menu options can be accessed from the keyboard with 'quick key' combinations which are shown on the drop-down menus. If a sub-menu option is not available, at any time, it will display in a grey colour. Some menu options only appear in Excel when that tool or command is being used.

Dialogue Boxes:

Three periods after a sub-menu option or command, means that a dialogue box will open when the option or command is selected. A dialogue box is used for the insertion of additional information, such as the name of a file or path.

To see a dialogue box, press <Alt+F>, and select the **Open** option. The 'Open' dialogue box is displayed, as shown below.

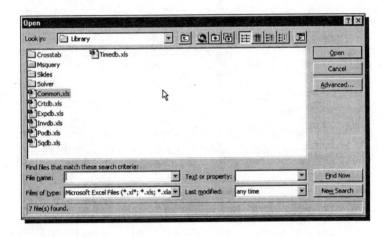

When a dialogue box opens, the easiest way to move around it is by clicking with the mouse, otherwise the <Tab> key can be used to move the cursor from one column in the box to another (<Shift+Tab> moves the cursor backwards). Alternatively you can move directly to a desired field by holding the <Alt> key down and pressing the underlined letter in the field name.

Within a column of options you must use the arrow keys to move from one to another. Having selected an option or typed in information, you must press a command button such as the **Open** or **Cancel** button, or choose from additional options.

To select the **Open** button with the mouse, simply point and click, while with the keyboard you must first press the <Tab> key until the dotted rectangle moves to the required button, and then press the <Enter> key. Pressing <Enter> at any time while a dialogue box is open, will cause the marked items to be selected and the box to be closed.

Some dialogue boxes contain List boxes which show a column of available choices, similar to the one at the top of the previous screen dump which appears by pressing the down-arrow button, as shown here. If there are more choices than can be seen in the area provided, use the scroll bars to reveal them. To select a single item from a List box, either double-click the item, or use the arrow keys to highlight the item and press <Enter>.

Other dialogue boxes contain Option buttons with a list of mutually exclusive items, as shown here. The default choice is marked with a black dot against its name, while unavailable options are dimmed. Other dialogue boxes contain Check boxes, like the one here, which offer a list of options you can switch on or off. Selected options show a tick in the box against the option name. If you want to see the above Option buttons and Check boxes, click the **Advanced** button of the Open dialogue box.

To cancel a dialogue box, either click the **Cancel** button, or press the <Esc> key. Pressing the <Esc> key in succession, closes one dialogue box at a time, and eventually aborts the menu option.

Workbook Navigation

When you first enter Excel, the program sets up a series of huge electronic pages, or worksheets, in your computer's memory, many times larger than the small part shown on the screen. Individual cells are identified by column and row location (in that order), with present size extending to 256 columns and 65,536 rows. The columns are labelled from A to Z, followed by AA to AZ, BA to BZ, and so on, to IV, while the rows are numbered from 1 to 65,536.

A worksheet can be thought of as a two-dimensional table made up of rows and columns. The point where a row and column intersect is called a cell, while the reference points of a cell are known as the cell address. The active cell (A1 when you first enter the program) is boxed. A workbook is made up of different worksheets stacked 'on top of each other'.

Navigation around a worksheet is achieved by using one of the following keys or key combinations:

- Pressing one of the four arrow keys (→↓←↑) moves the active cell one position right, down, left or up, respectively.

- Pressing the <PgDn> or <PgUp> keys moves the active cell down or up one visible page.

- Pressing the <Ctrl+→> or <Ctrl+↓> key combinations moves the active cell to the extreme right of the worksheet (column IV) or extreme bottom of the worksheet (row 65,536).

- Pressing the <Home> key, moves the active cell to the beginning of a row.

- Pressing the <Ctrl+Home> key combination moves the active cell to the home position, A1.

- Pressing the <Ctrl+End> key combination moves the active cell to the lower right corner of the worksheet's currently used area.

- Pressing the **F5** function key will display the Go To dialogue box shown below.

In the **Go to** box a list of named ranges in the active worksheet (to be discussed shortly) is displayed, or one of the last four references from which you chose the **Go To** command.

In the **Reference** box you type the cell reference or a named range you want to move to.

To move the active cell with a mouse, do the following:

- Point to the cell you want to move to and click the left mouse button. If the cell is not visible, move the window by clicking on the scroll bar arrowhead that points in the direction you want to move.

- To move a page at a time, click in the scroll bar itself.

- For larger moves, drag the box in the scroll bar, but the distances moved will depend on the size of the worksheet.

When you have finished navigating around the worksheet, press the <Ctrl+Home> key combination which will move the active cell to the A1 position (provided you have not fixed titles in any rows or columns or have no hidden rows or columns - more about these later).

Note that the area within which you can move the active cell is referred to as the working area of the worksheet, while the letters and numbers in the border at the top and left of the working area give the 'co-ordinates' of the cells in a worksheet.

The location of the active cell is constantly monitored by the 'selection indicator' which is to be found on the extreme left below the lower Toolbar of the application window. As the active cell is moved, this indicator displays its address, as shown below.

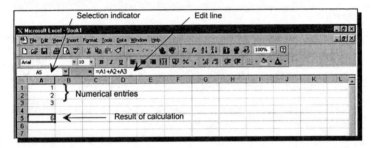

The contents of a cell are displayed above the column letters within what is known as the 'Edit line'. If you type text in the active cell, what you type appears in both the 'Edit line' and the cell itself.

Typing a formula which is preceded by the equals sign (=) to, say, add the contents of three cells, causes the actual formula to appear in the 'Edit line', while the result of the actual calculation appears in the active cell when the <Enter> key is pressed.

Moving Between Sheets:

You can scroll between sheets by clicking one of the arrows situated to the left of Sheet 1, as shown on the next page. We have labelled these as 'Tab scrolling buttons'. The inner arrows scroll sheets one at a time in the direction of the arrow, while the outer arrows scroll to the end, or beginning, of the group of available sheets. A sheet is then made current by clicking its tab.

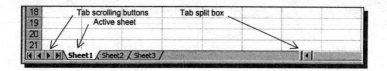

With the keyboard, you can scroll one sheet at a time, and make it active at the same time, by using the <Ctrl+PgDn> key combination. Using <Ctrl+PgUp> scrolls in the reverse direction.

To display more sheet tabs at a time, drag the split box to the right. The reverse action displays less sheet tabs. To rename sheets, double-click at their tab, then type a new name to replace the highlighted name of the particular sheet tab.

To insert a sheet in front of a certain sheet, make that sheet current, then use the **Insert, Worksheet** command sequence. To delete a sheet, make it current and use the **Edit, Delete Sheet** command sequence.

Rearranging Sheet Order:

If you need to rearrange the order in which sheets are being held in a workbook, you can do so by dragging a particular sheet to its new position, as shown below.

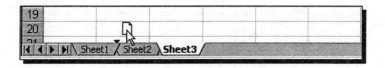

While you are dragging the tab of the sheet you want to move, the mouse pointer changes to an arrow pointing to a sheet. The small solid arrowhead to the left of the mouse pointer indicates the place where the sheet you are moving will be placed.

Grouping Worksheets:

You can select several sheets and group them together so that data entry, editing, or formatting can be made easier and more consistent.

To select adjacent sheets, click the first sheet tab, hold down the <Shift> key and then click the last sheet tab in the group. To select non-adjacent sheets, click the first sheet tab, hold down the <Ctrl> key and then click the other sheet tabs you want to group together.

Selecting sheets in the above manner, causes the word '[Group]' to appear in the Title bar of the active window, and the tabs of the selected sheets to be shown in white. To cancel the selection, click at the tab of any sheet which is not part of the selected group.

Selecting a Range of Cells:

To select a range of cells, say, A3:C3, point to cell A3, then

- press the left mouse button, and while holding it pressed, drag the mouse to the right.

To select a range from the keyboard, first make active the first cell in the range, then

- hold down the <Shift> key and use the right arrow key ($\rightarrow$) to highlight the required range.

To select a 3D range, across several sheets, select the range in the first sheet, then

- release the mouse button, hold down the <Shift> key, and click the Tab of the last sheet in the range.

Viewing Multiple Workbook Sheets

To see more clearly what you are doing when working with multiple workbook sheets, type the text '1st' in location A1 of Sheet1, the text '2nd' in Sheet2, and so on. Then use the **Window, New Window** command to add three extra windows to your worksheet so that you can view different parts of a sheet at the same time (to add extra sheets in a workbook, use the **Insert, Worksheet** command). Finally, use the **Window, Arrange, Tiled** command to display the four sheets as shown below.

To move from one window to another, simply point with the mouse to the cell of the window you want to go to and click the left mouse button. To display a different sheet in each window, go to a window and click the sheet's tab.

To return to single-window view mode from a tiled or cascade mode, click the maximise button of the active window.

33

Entering Information

We will now investigate how information can be entered into a worksheet. But first, make sure you are in Sheet1, then return to the Home (A1) position, by pressing the <Ctrl+Home> key combination, then type the words:

    PROJECT ANALYSIS

As you type, the characters appear in both the 'Edit line' and the active cell. If you make a mistake, press the <BkSp> key to erase the previous letter or the <Esc> key to start again. When you have finished, press <Enter>.

Note that what you have just typed in has been entered in cell A1, even though the whole of the word ANALYSIS appears to be in cell B1. If you use the right arrow key to move the active cell to B1 you will see that the cell is indeed empty.

Typing any letter at the beginning of an entry into a cell results in a 'text' entry being formed automatically, otherwise known as a 'label'. If the length of the text is longer than the width of a cell, it will continue into the next cell to the right of the current active cell, provided that cell is empty, otherwise the displayed information will be truncated.

To edit information already in a cell, either

- double-click the cell in question, or
- make that cell the active cell and press the **F2** function key.

The cursor keys, the <Home> and <End> keys, as well as the <Ins> and <Del> keys can be used to move the cursor and/or edit information as required.

You can also 'undo' the last 16 actions carried out since the program was last in the **Ready** mode, by either using the **Edit, Undo Entry** command or clicking the Undo button.

Next, move the active cell to B3 and type

```
Jan
```

Pressing the right arrow key (→) will automatically enter the typed information into the cell and also move the active cell one cell to the right, in this case to C3. Now type

```
Feb
```

and press <Enter>.

The looks of a worksheet can be enhanced somewhat by using different types of borders around specific cells. To do this, first select the range of cells, then click at the down arrow of the Borders icon on the Formatting Toolbar, shown here, which displays twelve different types of borders, as shown below.

In our example, we have selected the cell range A3:C3, then we chose the 8th border from the display table.

Next, move to cell A4 and type the label Income, then enter the numbers 14000 and 15000 in cells B4 and C4, respectively, as shown below, but note that by default the labels 'Jan' and 'Feb' are left justified, while the numbers are right justified.

	A	B	C	D	E	F	G	H
1	PROJECT ANALYSIS							
2								
3		Jan	Feb					
4	Income	14000	15000		✛			
5								

Changing Text Alignment and Fonts:

One way of improving the looks of this worksheet is to also right justify the text 'Jan' and 'Feb' within their respective cells. To do this, move the active cell to B3 and select the range B3 to C3 by dragging the mouse, then either click the 'Align Right' icon, shown here, or choose the

Format, Cells

command, then select the **Alignment** tab from the displayed Format Cells dialogue box, shown below, click the down-arrow against the **Horizontal** text box, highlight **Right** from the drop-down menu options, and press **OK**.

No matter which method you choose, the text labels should now appear right justified within their cells. Although the latter method is lengthier, it nevertheless provides you with greater flexibility in displaying text, both in terms of position and orientation.

We could further improve the looks of our worksheet by choosing a different font for the heading 'Project Analysis'. To achieve this, select cell A1, then click on the 'Font Size' button on the second Toolbar, to reveal the band of available point sizes for the selected font, as shown here. From this band, choose 14, then click in succession the 'Bold' and 'Italic' icons.

Finally, since the numbers in cells B4 to C4 represent money, it would be better if these were prefixed with the £ sign. To do this, select the cell range B4:C4, then either click the 'Currency Style' button on the second Toolbar, shown here, or choose the

F_ormat, _Style

command and select **Currency** from the list under **_Style Name** in the displayed Style dialogue box.

The numbers within the chosen range will now be displayed in currency form, provided the width of the cells is sufficient to accommodate them. In our example, the entered numbers are far too long to fit in currency form in the default cell width and appear as shown under the 'Feb' entry below.

To see the actual numbers, we must increase the width of the columns B4:C4 to 11 characters wide (as

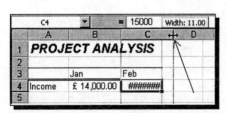

shown at the top right of the display within a pop-up text box). To do this, place the mouse pointer in between the column letters on the dividing line, and drag the pointer to the right, as pointed to above, until the width of the column is displayed as 11.00.

Shortcut Menus:

While a range of cells in a sheet is selected, or a group

of sheets is active, you can access a shortcut menu of relevant commands by pressing the right mouse button. This produces a shortcut menu, as shown here, of the most common commands relevant to what you are doing at the time.

Saving a Workbook

Now, let us assume that we would like to stop at this point, but would also like to save the work entered so far before leaving the program. First, return to the Home position by pressing <Ctrl+Home>. This is good practice because when a workbook is opened later, the position of the cell pointer at the time of saving the file appears at the top left corner of the opened worksheet, which might cause confusion if below and to the right of it there are no entries - you might think that you have opened an empty worksheet.

Next, choose the **File, Save** command to reveal the Save As dialogue box. You could select to save your work in the default **My Documents** folder, or on a floppy disc in the **a:** drive as we have done, or somewhere else - the choice is yours. Next, type the new name of the file, say, **Project 1** in the **File name** box. The file will be saved in the default file type *Microsoft Excel Workbook*, as displayed in the **Save as type** box. Excel adds the file extension **.xls** automatically, for identity, but normally you cannot see it.

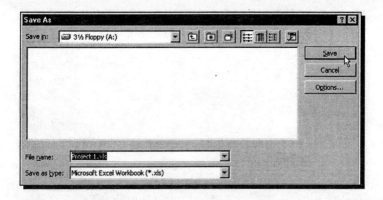

If you want to create backup files or provide password protection to your file, click the **Options** button. Clicking the **Save** button, causes the file to be saved under the chosen name.

Opening a Workbook

An already saved workbook, or file, can be opened by either clicking at the 'Open' icon, shown here, or selecting the

File, Open

command which displays the Open dialogue box, shown on the next page. Do not forget to change the drive to **a:**, if that is where you saved your work (by selecting 3½ Floppy (A:) in the **Look in** box drop-down list). Excel asks for a filename to open, with the default *Microsoft Excel Files* being displayed in the **Files of type** box, as shown below. If the file was saved, select it by clicking its name in the list box, then click the **Open** button.

If you haven't saved it, don't worry as you could just as easily start afresh.

If you want to change the logged drive, click the down-arrow against the **Look in** box, and select the appropriate drive from the drop-down list.

Exiting Excel

To exit Excel, close any displayed dialogue boxes by clicking the **Cancel** button, and make sure that the word **Ready** is displayed on the status bar (press the <Esc> key until it does), and either

- choose the **File, Exit** command,
- use the <Alt+F4> key combination, or
- click the Close button.

No matter which command you choose, if you have changed any opened worksheet, Excel will warn you and will ask for confirmation before exiting the program.

3. FILLING IN A WORKSHEET

We will use, as an example on how a worksheet can be built up, the few entries on 'Project Analysis' from the previous chapter. If you have saved **Project 1**, then either click the Open button, or use the **File, Open** command, then highlight its filename in the Open dialogue box, and click the **OK** button. If you haven't saved it, don't worry as you could just as easily start afresh.

Next, either double-click the contents of a cell to edit existing entries, or simply retype the contents of cells, so that your worksheet looks as near as possible to the one below. For formatting details, see below and the next page.

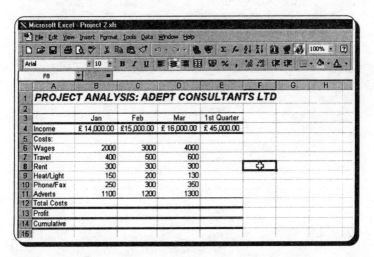

The lines, like the double line stretching from A3 to E3 were entered by first selecting the cell range A3:E3, then clicking the down-arrow of the 'Borders' icon on the second Toolbar, and selecting the appropriate border from the 12 displayed options.

Formatting Entries

The information in cell A1 (PROJECT ANALYSIS: ADEPT CONSULTANTS LTD) was entered left justified and formatted by clicking on the 'Font Size' button on the Formatting Toolbar, and selecting 14 point font size from the band of available font sizes, then clicking in succession the 'Bold' and 'Italic' icons.

The text in the cell block B3:E3 was formatted by first selecting the range and then clicking the 'Centre' alignment icon on the second Toolbar, so the text within the range was displayed centre justified.

The numbers within the cell block B4:E4 were formatted by first selecting the range, then clicking the 'Currency Style' icon on the second Toolbar, shown here, so the numbers appeared with two digits after the decimal point and prefixed with the £ sign.

All the text appearing in column A (apart from that in cell A1) was just typed in (left justified), as shown in the screen dump on the previous page.

Filling a Range by Example:

To fill a range by example, select the range, point at the bottom right corner of the selected range and when the mouse pointer changes to a small cross, drag the mouse in the required direction.

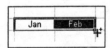

In the above case, the next cell to the right will automatically fill with the text 'Mar' (Excel anticipates that you want to fill cells by example with the abbreviations for months, and does it for you). Not only that, but it also copies the format of the selected range forward. It is, therefore, evident that selecting ranges and using icons makes various tasks a lot easier.

Entering Text, Numbers and Formulae:

Excel 97 allows you to format both text (labels) and numbers in any way you choose. For example, you can have numbers centre justified in their cells.

When text, a number, a formula, or an Excel function is entered into a cell, or reference is made to the contents of a cell by the cell address, then the content of the status bar changes from **Ready** to **Enter**. This status can be changed back to **Ready** by either completing an entry and pressing <Enter> or one of the arrow keys, or by pressing <Esc>.

We can find the 1st quarter total income from consultancy, by activating cell E4, typing

=B4+C4+D4

and pressing <Enter>. The total first quarter income is added, using the above formula, and the result is placed in cell E4.

Now complete the insertion into the spreadsheet of the various amounts under 'costs' and then choose the

File, Save As

command to save the resultant worksheet under the filename **Project 2**, before going on any further. Remember that saving your work on disc often enough is a good thing to get used to, as even the shortest power cut can cause the loss of hours of hard work!

Using Functions

In our example, writing a formula that adds the contents of three columns is not too difficult or lengthy a task. But imagine having to add 20 columns! For this reason Excel has an in-built summation function which can be used to add any number of columns (or rows).

To illustrate how this and other functions can be used,
activate cell E4 and press the Paste Function
button shown here. If the function you require
appears on the displayed dialogue box under
Function name, choose it, otherwise select the
appropriate class from the list under **Function
category**.

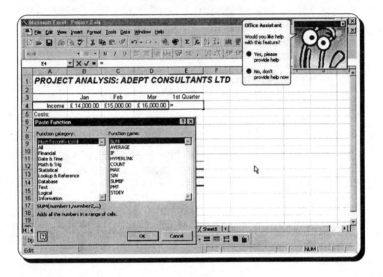

Choosing the **SUM** function, inserts the entry
SUM(B4:D4) in the Edit line, as shown below. Clicking
the **OK** button, causes this function to be pasted into
cell E4, adding all the numbers in the range.

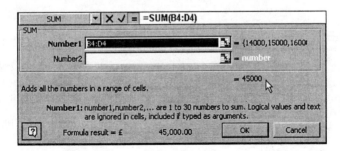

44

Using the AutoSum Icon:

With addition, there is a better and quicker way of letting Excel work out the desired result. To illustrate this, select the cell range B6:E12, which contains the 'Costs' we would like to add up. To add these in both the horizontal and vertical direction, we include in the selected range an empty column to the right of the numbers and an empty row below the numbers, as shown below.

	A	B	C	D	E	F	G	H
1	PROJECT ANALYSIS: ADEPT CONSULTANTS LTD							
2								
3		Jan	Feb	Mar	1st Quarter			
4	Income	£ 14,000.00	£15,000.00	£ 16,000.00	£ 45,000.00			
5	Costs:							
6	Wages	2000	3000	4000				
7	Travel	400	500	600				
8	Rent	300	300	300				
9	Heat/Light	150	200	130				
10	Phone/Fax	250	300	350				
11	Adverts	1100	1200	1300				
12	Total Costs							
13	Profit							

Pressing the 'AutoSum' icon, shown here, inserts the result of the summations in the empty column and row, as shown below. The selected range remains selected so that any other formatting can be applied by simply pressing the appropriate icon button.

	A	B	C	D	E	F	G	H
1	PROJECT ANALYSIS: ADEPT CONSULTANTS LTD							
2								
3		Jan	Feb	Mar	1st Quarter			
4	Income	£ 14,000.00	£15,000.00	£ 16,000.00	£ 45,000.00			
5	Costs:							
6	Wages	2000	3000	4000	9000			
7	Travel	400	500	600	1500			
8	Rent	300	300	300	900			
9	Heat/Light	150	200	130	480			
10	Phone/Fax	250	300	350	900			
11	Adverts	1100	1200	1300	3600			
12	Total Costs	4200	5500	6680	16380			

Now complete the insertion of formulae in the rest of the worksheet, noting that 'Profit', in B13, is the difference between 'Income' and 'Total Cost', calculated by the formula **=B4-B12**. To complete the entry, this formula should be copied using the 'fill by example' method into the three cells to its right.

The 'Cumulative' entry in cell B14 should be a simple reference to cell B13, that is **=B13**, while in cell C14 it should be **=B14+C13**. Similarly, the latter formula is copied into cell D14 using the 'fill by example' method.

Next, format the entire range B6:E12 by selecting the range and clicking the 'Currency' button.

If you make any mistakes and copy formats or information into cells you did not mean to, use the

Edit, Undo

command or click the Undo button which allows you to selectively undo what you were just doing. To blank the contents within a range of cells, first select the range, then press the <Del> key.

The worksheet, up to this point, should look as follows:

	A	B	C	D	E	F	G	H
1	*PROJECT ANALYSIS: ADEPT CONSULTANTS LTD*							
2								
3		Jan	Feb	Mar	1st Quarter			
4	Income	£ 14,000.00	£15,000.00	£ 16,000.00	£ 45,000.00			
5	Costs:							
6	Wages	£ 2,000.00	£ 3,000.00	£ 4,000.00	£ 9,000.00			
7	Travel	£ 400.00	£ 500.00	£ 600.00	£ 1,500.00			
8	Rent	£ 300.00	£ 300.00	£ 300.00	£ 900.00			
9	Heat/Light	£ 150.00	£ 200.00	£ 130.00	£ 480.00		⟳	
10	Phone/Fax	£ 250.00	£ 300.00	£ 350.00	£ 900.00			
11	Adverts	£ 1,100.00	£ 1,200.00	£ 1,300.00	£ 3,600.00			
12	Total Costs	£ 4,200.00	£ 5,500.00	£ 6,680.00	£ 16,380.00			
13	Profit	£ 9,800.00	£ 9,500.00	£ 9,320.00	£ 28,620.00			
14	Cumulative	£ 9,800.00	£19,300.00	£ 28,620.00				
15								

Finally, use the **File, Save As** command to save your work under the filename **Project 3**.

Printing a Worksheet

To print a worksheet, make sure that the printer you propose to use was defined when you first installed Windows.

If you have named more than one printer in your original installation of Windows, and want to select a printer other than your original first choice, then select the **File, Print** command, click the down-arrow against the **Name** box on the displayed Print dialogue box and select the required printer, as shown below.

If you want to change the paper size, print orientation or printer resolution, click the **Properties** button on the Print dialogue box. These and other changes to the appearance of the printout can also be made by choosing the **File, Page Setup** command which causes the Page Setup dialogue box to be displayed, as shown overleaf.

By selecting the appropriate Tab on this dialogue box, you can change your **Page** settings, page **Margins**, specify a **Header/Footer**, and control how a **Sheet** should be printed. Each Tab displays a different dialogue box, appropriate to the function at hand. In the **Header/Footer** dialogue box you can even click the down-arrow against the Header and Footer boxes to display a suggested list for these, appropriate to the work you are doing, the person responsible for it and even the date it is being carried out! Try it.

A very useful feature of Excel is the **Scaling** facility shown in the above dialogue box. You can print actual size or a percentage of it, or you can choose to fit your worksheet on to one page which allows Excel to scale your work automatically.

To preview a worksheet, click the 'Print Preview' icon on the Toolbar, shown here, or click the **Print Preview** button on the Page Setup dialogue box, or the **Preview** button on the Print dialogue box. You can even use the **File, Print Preview** command!

The idea of all these preview choices is to make it easy for you to see your work on screen before committing it to paper, thus saving a few more trees!

Enhancing a Worksheet

You can make your work look more professional by adopting various enhancements, such as single and double line cell borders, shading certain cells, and adding meaningful headers and footers.

However, with Excel you can easily select a pre-defined style to display your work on both the screen and on paper. To do this, place the active cell within the table (or range) you want to format, say C5, then select the **Format, AutoFormat** which will cause the following dialogue box to appear on the screen, displaying a sample of the chosen table format. In this way you can choose what best suits your needs. We selected 'Classic 2' and pressed **OK**.

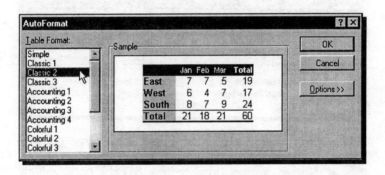

Next, reduce the title of the worksheet to PROJECT ANALYSIS, then centre it within the range A1:E1, by first selecting the range, then clicking the 'Merge and Centre' icon, shown here, which causes the title to centre within the specified range.

Finally, save the worksheet as **Project 4**, before going on.

Header and Footer Icons and Codes:

With the help of header and footer icons and their codes, shown below, you can position text or automatically insert information at the top or bottom of a report printout.

To add a header to our printed example, use the **File, Page Setup** command and click first the **Header/Footer** Tab, then the **Custom Header** button and type the information displayed below in the **Left section** and **Right section** of the Header box.

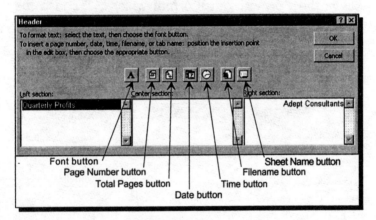

While the insertion pointer is in, say, the **Centre section** of the Header box, pointing and clicking on the 'Sheet Name' button, inserts the &[Tab] code which has the effect of inserting the sheet name of the current active sheet at the time of printing. The first icon button displays the Font dialogue box, while the others display the following codes:

Code	*Action*
&[Page]	Inserts a page number.
&[Pages]	Inserts the total number of pages.
&[Date]	Inserts the current date.
&[Time]	Inserts the current time.
&[File]	Inserts the filename of the current workbook.

Setting a Print Area:

To choose a smaller print area than the current worksheet, select the required area by highlighting the starting cell of the area and dragging the mouse, or using the **<Shift+Arrows>**, to highlight the block, and use the **File, Print** command which displays the following dialogue box:

Choose the **Selection** button in the **Print what** box, and either click the **Preview** or the **OK** button to preview your report on screen or print it on paper. Once in preview mode, the following icons are available to you.

The first two allow you to change sheets, while the next one allows you to review your print output magnified or at full page size - when in full page size, the mouse pointer looks like a magnifying glass, as above. The next four icons can be used to print, change page settings, display and change the margins, or adjust the page size by dragging the page breaks to a new position. To return to normal view, click the **Close** button.

Another way to set the area to print is using the **File, Print Area, Set Print Area** menu command. To print selected sheets or the entire workbook, click the appropriate button in the **Print what** box of the Print dialogue box.

The default selection in the **Print what** box is **Active sheet(s)** which is also what will be printed out if you click the 'Print' icon, shown here. If you have included headers and footers, these will be printed out irrespective of whether you choose to print a selected range or a selected worksheet. To centre the page horizontally on the paper, use the **File, Page Setup** command, click the Margins tab and select the option. Finally, printing our worksheet, produces the following page:

	Jan	Feb	Mar	1st Quarter
Income	£14,000.00	£15,000.00	£16,000.00	£45,000.00
Costs:				
Wages	£ 2,000.00	£ 3,000.00	£ 4,000.00	£ 9,000.00
Travel	£ 400.00	£ 500.00	£ 600.00	£ 1,500.00
Rent	£ 300.00	£ 300.00	£ 300.00	£ 900.00
Heat/Light	£ 150.00	£ 200.00	£ 130.00	£ 480.00
Phone/Fax	£ 250.00	£ 300.00	£ 350.00	£ 900.00
Adverts	£ 1,100.00	£ 1,200.00	£ 1,300.00	£ 3,600.00
Total Costs	£ 4,200.00	£ 5,500.00	£ 6,680.00	£16,380.00
Profit	£ 9,800.00	£ 9,500.00	£ 9,320.00	£28,620.00
Cumulative	£ 9,800.00	£19,300.00	£28,620.00	

Quarterly Profits

Adept Consultants

10/6/97

Page 1

3-Dimensional Worksheets

In Excel 97, a Workbook is a 3-dimensional file made up with a series of flat 2-dimensional sheets stacked 'on top of each other'. Each sheet is the same size, and in itself, behaves the same as the more ordinary worksheets. As mentioned previously, each separate sheet in a file has its own Tab identifier at the bottom of the screen. Ranges can be set to span several different sheets to build up 3-dimensional blocks of data. These blocks can then be manipulated, copied, or moved to other locations in the file. A cell can reference any other cell in the file, no matter what sheet it is on, and an extended range of functions can be used to process these 3-dimensional ranges.

Manipulating Ranges:

The best way to demonstrate a new idea is to work through an example - we will use the worksheet saved under **Project 4**. Next, start Excel, use the **File, Open** command, or click the File Open icon, and select **Project 4**. On pressing <Enter>, the worksheet should be displayed on the screen as shown on the facing page.

Copying Sheets in a Workbook:

We will now fill another three sheets behind the present one, in order to include information about ADEPT Consultants' trading during the other three quarters of the year. The easiest way of doing this is by copying the information in Sheet1, including the formatting and the entered formulae, onto the other three sheets, then edit the numerical information in these appropriately.

To simplify this operation, Excel has a facility which allows you to copy a sheet into a workbook. There are two ways of doing this: (a) with the mouse, or (b) using the menus.

With the mouse, make the sheet you want to copy the current sheet, then press the <Ctrl> key, and while keeping it pressed, point with the mouse on the Tab of Sheet1 and drag it to the right, as follows:

A small black triangle indicates the place where the copy will be inserted. If you insert a copy, say before Sheet2, when you release the mouse button the inserted sheet will be given the name Sheet1(2), as shown above, where we are about to insert a second copy before Sheet2 which will be named Sheet1(3).

To copy a sheet with the menus, select the **Edit, Move or Copy Sheet** command, then highlight Sheet2 in the **Before sheet** list of the displayed dialogue box, then check the **Create a copy** option at the bottom of the dialogue box, and press the **OK** button. Sheet1(2) will be inserted in the Workbook, in the above case.

When you have three copies placed, double-click the Tabs of Sheet1 and the three new sheets and change their names to 'Quarter 1', 'Quarter 2', 'Quarter 3' and 'Quarter 4', respectively. The contents of the second sheet should be as follows:

	A	B	C	D	E	F
1	**PROJECT ANALYSIS 2nd Quarter**					
2						
3		Apr	May	Jun	2nd Quarter	
4	Income	£ 15,500.00	£ 16,000.00	£ 16,500.00	£ 48,000.00	
5	Costs:					
6	Wages	£ 3,500.00	£ 4,000.00	£ 4,500.00	£ 12,000.00	
7	Travel	£ 500.00	£ 550.00	£ 580.00	£ 1,630.00	
8	Rent	£ 300.00	£ 300.00	£ 300.00	£ 900.00	
9	Heat/Light	£ 150.00	£ 120.00	£ 100.00	£ 370.00	
10	Phone/Fax	£ 300.00	£ 350.00	£ 400.00	£ 1,050.00	
11	Adverts	£ 1,250.00	£ 1,300.00	£ 1,350.00	£ 3,900.00	
12	Total Costs	£ 6,000.00	£ 6,620.00	£ 7,230.00	£ 19,850.00	
13	*Profit*	£ 9,500.00	£ 9,380.00	£ 9,270.00	£ 28,150.00	
14	*Cumulative*	£ 9,500.00	£ 18,880.00	£ 28,150.00		
15						
16						
17						
18						

Quarter 1 \ **Quarter 2** / Quarter 3 / Quarter 4 / Sheet2

The easiest way to enter these 2nd Quarter results is to edit the copied data (from Quarter 1) by either using the EDIT key (**F2**), or double-clicking the cell you want to edit. You should now be in a position to complete editing this sheet. Be extra careful, from now on, to check the identification Tab at the bottom of the screen, so as not to get the sheets mixed up. You do not want to spend time editing the wrong worksheet!

After building up the four worksheets (one for each quarter - see below for details on the 3rd and 4th quarters) save the file as **Project 5**.

	Jul	Aug	Sep	Oct	Nov	Dec
Income	17,000	17,500	18,000	18,500	19,000	19,500
Costs:						
Wages	4,000	4,500	5,000	4,500	5,000	5,500
Travel	600	650	680	630	670	700
Rent	300	300	300	300	300	300
Heat/Light	50	80	120	160	200	250
Phone/Fax	350	380	420	400	420	450
Adverts	1,400	1,450	1,500	1,480	1,500	1,530

Linking Sheets

A consolidation sheet could be placed in front of our 'stack' of data sheets to show a full year's results, by making a copy of the 1st Quarter sheet and placing it in front of it. Next, delete the entries in columns B to E, and name it 'Consolidation'.

We are now in a position to link the consolidation sheet to the other quarterly data sheets so that the information contained on them is automatically summarised and updated on it. The quarter totals in columns E of sheets Quarter 1, Quarter 2, Quarter 3, and Quarter 4, can be copied in turn to the clipboard using the **Edit, Copy** command, and then pasted to the appropriate column of the Consolidation sheet with the use of the **Edit, Paste Special** command and clicking the **Paste Link** button on the displayed dialogue box.

Note: Empty cells linked with this method, like those in cells E5 of each quarter, appear as 0 (zero) in the Consolidation sheet, and cannot be removed. To correct this, copy each column E of each quarter in two stages; E3:E4, then E6:E13.

Next, insert appropriate formulae in row 14 to correctly calculate the cumulative values in the Consolidation sheet. The result should be as follows:

	E13		=('Quarter 4'!$E$6:$E$13)					
	A	B	C	D	E	F	G	H
1		PROJECT ANALYSIS - Year Summary						
2								
3		1st Quarter	2nd Quarter	3rd Quarter	4th Quarter			
4	Income	£ 45,000.00	£ 48,000.00	£ 52,500.00	£ 57,000.00			
5	Costs:							
6	Wages	£ 9,000.00	£ 12,000.00	£ 13,500.00	£ 15,000.00			
7	Travel	£ 1,500.00	£ 1,630.00	£ 1,930.00	£ 2,000.00			
8	Rent	£ 900.00	£ 900.00	£ 900.00	£ 900.00			
9	Heat/Light	£ 480.00	£ 370.00	£ 250.00	£ 610.00			
10	Phone/Fax	£ 900.00	£ 1,050.00	£ 1,150.00	£ 1,270.00			
11	Adverts	£ 3,600.00	£ 3,900.00	£ 4,350.00	£ 4,510.00			
12	Total Costs	£ 16,380.00	£ 19,850.00	£ 22,080.00	£ 24,290.00			
13	Profit	£ 28,620.00	£ 28,150.00	£ 30,420.00	£ 32,710.00			
14	Cumulative	£ 28,620.00	£ 56,770.00	£ 87,190.00	£119,900.00			

Finally, save the resultant workbook as **Project 6**.

Linking Files

In the last example we built a consolidation report on a separate sheet in front of several parallel data sheets. All these sheets were, however, part of the same file. There may be times, however, when the consolidation data would be preferable in a separate file. As an example of linking files, we will work through an exercise to carry out this operation.

File Commands:

Use the **File, Close** command to close **Project 6** and clear the computer's memory, and **File, Open** to open **Project 5**. Next, place another empty file in memory using the **File, New** command. You can tell that a new file has been created, because the filename Book2 appears on the Title bar.

We would like to paste links between columns E of each quarter sheet of file **Project 5** and the newly opened file. This is best done if both files can be viewed at the same time, so use the **Window, Arrange, Tiled** command, then copy all the labels from sheet Quarter 1 of the file **Project 5** onto Sheet1 of the new file using the **Edit, Copy** and **Edit, Paste Special** command. The result so far should be as follows:

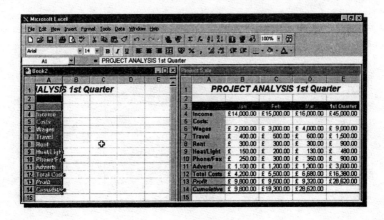

57

Note that the only difference between the styles of the two files is that the column widths have not transferred across when copying in this manner, therefore adjust them to a width of 11. Also the contents of cell A1 are

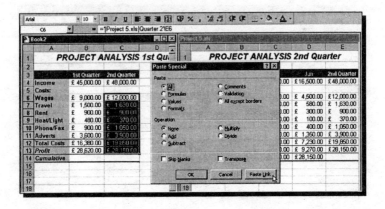

not centred within the range A1:E1, as they should be. To do so, highlight the range and click the Merge and Centre icon shown here.

Copying between files is the same as copying between the separate sheets of a file. However, here we would like to paste both the formats of the cells, and the links, therefore a two-fold copy and paste process is necessary. First, select in turn each quarter's totals from **Project 5** (cells E3:E14 of each sheet), use the **Edit, Copy** command, and paste the formats with the **Edit, Paste Special** command, clicking the **Formats** button on the displayed dialogue box, and pressing **OK**.

Next, select each contiguous part of each quarter separately (to avoid pasting zeros where spaces should appear), copy them, and paste them with file links onto Sheet1 of the new file in columns B to E, using the **Edit, Paste Special** command and pressing the **Paste Link** button on the displayed dialogue box. Below we show this process in action when the second quarter has just been linked to Sheet1 of Book2, but with the Paste Special dialogue box also open.

Below we show the maximised consolidated file for all four quarters.

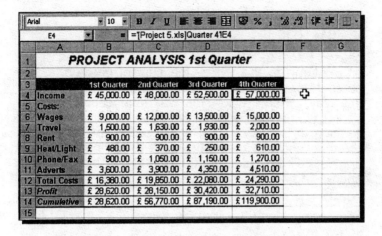

Note how cell references between different files (which could have been typed in) are shown with the filename and sheet name included in single quotes ('...'), placed before the cell address, if the sheet name includes a space. For example

='[Project 5.xls]Quarter 4'!E4

which implies that both files are on the drive and path.

If, however, **Project 5** was on a different drive, say D: and in the \DATA folder, then the above formula would be given as:

='D:\DATA\[Project 5.xls]Quarter 4'!E4

Next, add the appropriate formulae in row 14 to calculate the cumulative profits, and change the width of column E to 11.5 to accommodate the rather large year's end cumulative value. Finally, change the contents of cell A1 from 'PROJECT ANALYSIS 1st Quarter' to 'PROJECT ANALYSIS - Year Summary', before saving the linked books as **Adept 1**.

Relative and Absolute Cell Addresses

Entering a mathematical expression into Excel, such as the formula in cell C14 which was

=B14+C13

causes Excel to interpret it as 'add the contents of cell one column to the left of the current position, to the contents of cell one row above the current position'. In this way, when the formula was later copied into cell address D14, the contents of the cell relative to the left position of D14 (i.e. C14) and the contents of the cell one row above it (i.e. D13) were used, instead of the original cell addresses entered in C14. This is relative addressing.

To see the effect of relative versus absolute addressing, copy the formula in cell C14 into C17, as shown below:

C17	▼	= =B17+C16			
A	B	C	D	E	F
1		PROJECT ANALYSIS - Year Summary			
2					
3		1st Quarter	2nd Quarter	3rd Quarter	4th Quarter
4 Income	£ 45,000.00	£ 48,000.00	£ 52,500.00	£ 57,000.00	
5 Costs:					
6 Wages	£ 9,000.00	£ 12,000.00	£ 13,500.00	£ 15,000.00	
7 Travel	£ 1,500.00	£ 1,630.00	£ 1,930.00	£ 2,000.00	
8 Rent	£ 900.00	£ 900.00	£ 900.00	£ 900.00	
9 Heat/Light	£ 480.00	£ 370.00	£ 250.00	£ 610.00	
10 Phone/Fax	£ 900.00	£ 1,050.00	£ 1,150.00	£ 1,270.00	
11 Adverts	£ 3,600.00	£ 3,900.00	£ 4,350.00	£ 4,510.00	
12 Total Costs	£ 16,380.00	£ 19,850.00	£ 22,080.00	£ 24,290.00	
13 Profit	£ 28,620.00	£ 28,150.00	£ 30,420.00	£ 32,710.00	
14 Cumulative	£ 28,620.00	£ 56,770.00	£ 87,190.00	£119,900.00	
15					
16					
17		£ -	✛		

Note that in cell C14 the formula was =B14+C13. However, when copied into cell C17 the formula appears as

=B17+C16

because it has been interpreted as relative addressing. In this case, no value appears in cell C17 because we are attempting to add two blank cells.

Now change the formula in C14 by editing it to

=$B$14+$C$13

which is interpreted as absolute addressing. Copying this formula into cell C17 calculates the correct result. Highlight cell C17 and observe the cell references in its formula; they have not changed from those of cell C14.

The $ sign must prefix both the column reference and the row reference. Mixed cell addressing is permitted; as for example when a column address reference is needed to be taken as absolute, while a row address reference is needed to be taken as relative. In such a case, the column letter is prefixed by the $ sign.

When building an absolute cell reference in a formula, it is easier to select the cell with the mouse pointer and keep pressing the **F4** key until the correct $ prefix is set.

Freezing Panes on Screen

Sometimes there might be too much information on screen and attempting to see a certain part of a sheet might cause the labels associated with that information to scroll off the screen.

To freeze column (or row) labels of a worksheet on screen, move the cell pointer to the right (or below) the column (or row) which you want to freeze, and use the

Window, Freeze Panes

command. Everything to the left of (or above) the cell pointer will freeze on the screen.

In the example below, the cell pointer was placed in cell B4 of the **Adept 1** workbook, before issuing the command to freeze the panes. As seen on the screen dump, Excel added a vertical line between columns A and B, and a horizontal line between rows 3 and 4. Scrolling horizontally or vertically leaves column A and rows 1-3 always on screen.

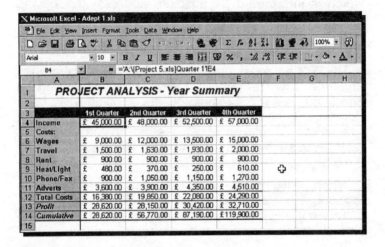

To remove unwanted frozen panes, or move their position on the worksheet, use the

Window, Unfreeze Panes

command.

4. SPREADSHEET CHARTS

Excel allows information within a worksheet to be represented in graphical form, which makes data more accessible to non-expert users who might not be familiar with the spreadsheet format. The saying 'a picture is worth a thousand words', applies equally well to charts and figures.

The package allows the use of several chart and graph types, including area, bar, column, line, doughnut, radar, XY, pie, combination, and several 3-D options of these charts. In all, Excel allows fourteen different types of charts, with almost 100 pre-defined formats, which can be selected by using the appropriate icon. These are made available to you once you have selected the data you want to chart and clicked on the Chart Wizard button on the toolbar.

Charts (you can have several per worksheet) can be displayed on screen at the same time as the worksheet from which they were derived, since they appear in their own 'chart' frame and can be embedded anywhere on a worksheet. Furthermore, they can be sent to an appropriate output device, such as a plotter or printer. Although this charting module rivals a standalone graphics package, and one could write a separate book on it, an attempt will be made to present its basics, in the space available within this book.

Preparing for a Column Chart

In order to illustrate some of the graphing capabilities of Excel, we will now plot the income of the consulting company we discussed in the **Project 6** file. However, before we can go on, you will need to complete the entries for the last two quarters of trading of the Adept Consultants' example, if you haven't already done so - see end of previous chapter.

Next, link the quarterly totals to the consolidation sheet, calculate the year's total, as shown below, and save the resultant workbook as **Project 7**, before going on.

	F4		= =SUM(B4:E4)				
	A	B	C	D	E	F	G
1	*PROJECT ANALYSIS - Year Summary*						
2							
3		1st Quarter	2nd Quarter	3rd Quarter	4th Quarter	Total	
4	Income	£ 45,000.00	£ 48,000.00	£ 52,500.00	£ 57,000.00	£202,500.00	
5	Costs:						
6	Wages	£ 9,000.00	£ 12,000.00	£ 13,500.00	£ 15,000.00	£ 49,500.00	
7	Travel	£ 1,500.00	£ 1,630.00	£ 1,930.00	£ 2,000.00	£ 7,060.00	
8	Rent	£ 900.00	£ 900.00	£ 900.00	£ 900.00	£ 3,600.00	
9	Heat/Light	£ 480.00	£ 370.00	£ 250.00	£ 610.00	£ 1,710.00	
10	Phone/Fax	£ 900.00	£ 1,050.00	£ 1,150.00	£ 1,270.00	£ 4,370.00	
11	Adverts	£ 3,600.00	£ 3,900.00	£ 4,350.00	£ 4,510.00	£ 16,360.00	
12	Total Costs	£ 16,380.00	£ 19,850.00	£ 22,080.00	£ 24,290.00	£ 82,600.00	
13	Profit	£ 28,620.00	£ 28,150.00	£ 30,420.00	£ 32,710.00	£119,900.00	
14	Cumulative	£ 28,620.00	£ 56,770.00	£ 87,190.00	£119,900.00		
15							

`|◀ ◀ ▶ ▶|` \Consolidation ⟋ Quarter 1 ⟍ Quarter 2 ⟍ Quarter 3 ⟍ Quar `◀` |

Now we need to select the range of the data we want to graph. The range of data to be graphed in Excel does not have to be contiguous for each graph, as with some other spreadsheets. With Excel, you select your data from different parts of a sheet with the <Ctrl> key pressed down. This method has the advantage of automatic recalculation should any changes be made to the original data. You could also collect data from different sheets to one 'graphing' sheet by linking them as we did with the consolidation sheet.

If you don't want the chart to be recalculated when you do this, then you must use the **Edit, Copy** and **Edit, Paste Special** commands and choose the **Values** option from the displayed dialogue box, which copies a selected range to a specified target area of the worksheet and converts formulae to values. This is necessary, as cells containing formulae cannot be pasted directly since it would cause the relative cell addresses to adjust to the new locations; each formula would then recalculate a new value for each cell and give wrong results.

The Chart Wizard

To obtain a chart of 'Income' versus 'Quarters', select the data in cell range A3..E4, then either click the Chart Wizard button, shown here, or use the **Insert, Chart** command. The Chart Wizard then opens the first of four dialogue boxes, as shown below, which guide you through the process.

Now select the 3-D Column type and click the **Next >** button at the bottom of the displayed Chart Wizard dialogue box (not shown above). The second dialogue box is then displayed as follows, after clicking the **Columns** radio button pointed to below.

The third Chart Wizard dialogue box allows you to give a title to your chart and annotate the x- and y-axes, while the fourth dialogue box allows you to place the chart either on a separate sheet or on the sheet that was active when you first started the charting process. On pressing the **Finish** button the following chart should appear on your worksheet.

	1st Quarter	2nd Quarter	3rd Quarter	4th Quarter
Income	£ 45,000.00	£ 48,000.00	£ 52,500.00	£ 57,000.00

Note that to find out the exact details of a given column on a chart, you need only place the mouse pointer on it to cause a banner to appear with the desired information.

While the frame containing a chart is selected (you can tell from the presence of the small black squares around it), you can change its size by dragging the small two-headed arrow pointer (which appears when the mouse pointer is placed on the small black squares of the frame). You can also move the frame and its contents to another position on the worksheet by pointing to the chart area, pressing and keeping depressed the left mouse button until the pointer changes to a small four-headed arrow shape, then dragging the changed mouse pointer to a new position.

As an example of what you can do with a chart, let us first select it, then either double-click within the chart area or use the **Format, Selected Chart Area** command to obtain the following dialogue box:

From this dialogue box you can choose a pattern to be used as a frame, by selecting **Custom** under the Patterns tab and choose the 7th **Style**, the 4th **Weight** line, check the **Shadow** box and press **OK**.

Try it, then change the first quarter income from £45,000 to £55,000 (on the Quarter 1 sheet), and watch how the change is reflected on the redrawn graph on the Consolidation sheet displayed below.

You can change the type of chart shown on screen by first selecting it, then using the **Chart, Chart Type** command to display the first Chart Wizard dialogue box.

Finally, revert to the original entry for the first quarter's income, change your chart back to a simple column type, and then save your work again under the filename **Project 7** by simply pressing the Save icon shown here. Your current work will be saved to disc replacing the previous version under the same filename.

When Excel creates a chart, it plots each row or column of data in the selected range as a 'data series', such as a group of bars, lines, etc. A chart can contain many data series, but Excel charts data according to the following rules:

1.   If the selected range contains more rows than columns of data, Excel plots the data series by columns.

2.   If the selected range contains more columns than rows of data, or the same number of columns and rows, Excel plots the data series by rows.

If you select a range to chart which includes column and row headings, and text above or to the left of the numeric data, Excel uses the text to create the axis labels, legends, and title.

If your data selection does not obey these rules, you must tell Excel how your data series is structured in the 2nd Chart Wizard dialogue box.

Editing a Chart:

The easiest way to edit a chart is to right-click it while pointing within the chart area, but near its outer rim. This displays the shortcut menu shown here. As a chart is made up of several objects, for example, data series, plot area, the various axis data area, legends, and chart area, you will get a different shortcut menu if you were pointing to these different areas. Try it. As you right-click different areas, their name will appear in the 'Name box' which is situated below the 'Font' box. The shortcut menu shown here is the one you will get when you right-click the 'Chart Area'.

We have already used the first menu option to format our chart. The second menu option allows you to quickly change the chart type, while the third option can be used to change the source data. The fourth menu option allows you to add Titles, change axes, add grid lines and data labels, while the fifth option lets you specify whether you want your chart to be located in a new sheet or where you created.

Saving Charts:

When you save a workbook, the chart or charts you have created are saved with it. It is, therefore, a good idea not only to give each chart a title, but to also locate it on a differently named sheet.

Use the **Chart Options** in the above shortcut menu to give this chart the title **Yearly Income**, and the **Location** option to put the chart on a separate sheet and give it the name **Income Bar**. Finally, save the workbook under the filename **Project 8**.

Pre-defined Chart Types

To select a different type of chart, click the Chart Wizard icon shown here, or select the **Insert, Chart** command. The 1st Chart Wizard dialogue box displayed previously, lists 14 different chart options. These chart-types are normally used to describe the following relationships between data:

Area: for showing a volume relationship between two series, such as production or sales, over a given length of time.

Bar: for comparing differences in data (non-continuous data that are not related over time) by depicting changes in horizontal bars to show positive and negative variations from a given position.

Bubble: for showing a type of XY (scatter) chart. The size of the data (radius of the bubble) indicates the value of a third variable.

Column: for comparing separate items (non-continuous data which are related over time) by depicting changes in vertical bars to show positive and negative variations from a given position.

Cone: for showing 3-D column and bar charts in a more dramatic way.

Cylinder: similar to Cone.

Doughnut: for comparing parts with the whole. Similar to pie charts, but can depict more than one series of data.

Line: for showing continuous changes in data with time.

Pie: for comparing parts with the whole. You can use this type of chart when you want to compare the percentage of an item from a single series of data with the whole series.

Pyramid: similar to Cone.

Radar: for plotting one series of data as angle values defined in radians, against one or more series defined in terms of a radius.

Surface: for showing optimum combinations between two sets of data, as in a topographic map. Colours and patterns indicate areas that are in the same range of values.

Stock: for showing high-low-close type of data variation to illustrate stock market prices or temperature changes.

XY: for showing scatter relationships between X and Y. Scatter charts are used to depict items which are not related over time.

You can change the type of chart by selecting one of the fourteen alternate chart types from the 1st Chart Wizard dialogue box, provided your data fits the selection.

Customising a Chart

In order to customise a chart, you need to know how to add legends, titles, text labels, arrows, and how to change the colour and pattern of the chart background, plot areas and chart markers, and how to select, move and size chart objects.

Drawing a Multiple Column Chart:

As an exercise, we will consider a new column chart which deals with the quarterly 'Costs' of Adept Consultants. To achieve this, first select the Consolidation sheet of workbook **Project 8**, then highlight the cell range A3:E3, press the <Ctrl> key, and while holding it down, use the mouse to select the costs range A6:E11.

Next, click the Chart Wizard icon (or use the **Insert, Chart** command), select Column from the **Chart type** list, click the fourth **Chart sub-type** option, and press the **Next** button. The 6 different quarterly costs will be drawn automatically, as displayed in the composite screen dump below.

Because the selected range contains more rows than columns of data, Excel follows the 1st rule of data series selection which, however, might not be what you want.

To have the 'quarters' appearing on the x-axis and the 'costs' as the legends, we need to tell Excel that our data series is in rows by clicking the **Rows** button on the 2nd Chart Wizard dialogue box. Immediately this is done the column chart changes to:

The chart title and axes titles were inserted by typing the heading 'PROJECT ANALYSIS - Year Summary' in the **Chart title** box of the 3rd Chart Wizard dialogue box, followed by the **Axis Titles** shown above.

Once you are satisfied with your efforts, click the **As new sheet** radio button of the 4th Chart Wizard dialogue box, and name your chart **Costs Bar**. If you make a mistake and you want to try again, make sure the unwanted chart is selected, then press the <Del> key. Finally, save your work under the filename **Project 9**.

Changing a Title and an Axis Label:

To change a title, an axis label, or a legend within a chart, click the appropriate area on the chart. This reveals that these are individual objects (they are surrounded by small black squares) and you can edit, re-position them, or change their font and point size.

You can even rotate text within such areas in any direction you like.

To demonstrate these options, we will use the **Costs Bar** chart saved in **Project 9**, so get it on screen if you are to follow our suggestions.

To change the font size of a chart title, click the Chart Title area to select it and double-click on the border that is displayed when you select such an object. Doing this, displays the Format dialogue box for the selected object, and clicking the Font tab reveals the following:

From here, we changed the font size of the chart title from 10 to 16 points. We also selected the Costs label and changed its size to 14 points, then clicked the Alignment tab to change its orientation to 90°, as shown on the next page.

Drawing a Pie Chart:

To change the chart type, simply select the chart, then click the Chart Wizard and choose the 3-D Pie chart from the displayed list. If the selected chart was the 'quarterly costs' chart, then clicking the **Next** button and pressing the Series tab of the displayed dialogue box, shows the chart type that would be redrawn for the specified data series, as below.

In our case, the pie chart for the 1st Quarter is displayed in the dialogue box. Other quarters could be selected. However, so as not to spoil your **Costs Bar** chart, click the **Cancel** button at this stage.

To obtain a different pie chart, you must select the data range again, then click the Chart Wizard, choose the pie chart from the displayed chart types, then select the specific pie chart that best fits your data, specify the type of series, and give the chart a title.

As a last example in chart drawing, we will use the data ranges A6:A11 and F6:F11 of the Consolidation worksheet to plot a 3-D pie chart. The steps are the same as before, but for the 3-D option and specifying the type of series data as 'columns'. Note that the chart title should now reflect the Year Totals, rather than the Quarter summaries. The result should be as follows:

To display the above chart, we clicked the Data Labels tab and the **Show label and percent** radio button in the 3rd dialogue box of the Chart Wizard.

This chart tells us, for example, that Wages for the whole year amount to 60% of the total yearly costs. Other cost categories are also displayed with their appropriate percentages. Clicking the **Finish** button displays the pie chart in its finished form, as shown below.

Pointing to any pie slice, causes the pop-up poster to be displayed, informing you of the actual data series, its value and its percentage of the whole. It is now obvious that the information contained in this chart is much more than in the 2-D version.

If you want to explode an individual pie slice, you can do so by simply dragging it. This is possible as each slice is treated as a separate object, but you may have to increase the size of your chart before you can accurately pinpoint the required slice.

Finally, use the **Chart, Location** menu command to name this last version of the pie chart as **Costs Pie** and save your workbook.

The Drawing Tools

As long as you have a mouse, you can use Excel's Drawing tools (also known as Office Art tools) at the bottom of the screen. If this facility is not activated click
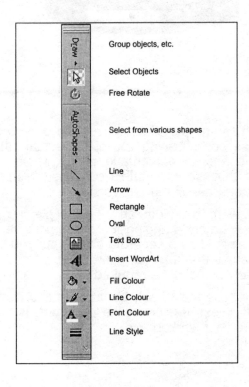
the Drawing button on the Toolbar, shown here, or use the **View, Toolbars, Drawing** command. You can use the Drawing tools to create, or edit, a graphic consisting of lines, arcs, ellipses, rectangles, and even text boxes. These can either exist in their own right, or be additions to a picture or object.

The various buttons on the Office Art toolbar have the following functions (see also next page):

Draw	Group objects, etc.
	Select Objects
	Free Rotate
AutoShapes	Select from various shapes
	Line
	Arrow
	Rectangle
	Oval
	Text Box
	Insert WordArt
	Fill Colour
	Line Colour
	Font Colour
	Line Style

Office Art:

Office Art is the new drawing tool shared by all Office 97 applications and gives Excel 97 a superior graphics capability. New or enhanced features are:

AutoShapes – the additional AutoShape categories, such as connectors, block arrows, flowchart symbols, stars and banners, callouts, and action buttons make drawing diagrams much easier.

Bezier curves – used to easily create exact curves with pin-point precision.

3-D effects – allow you to transform 2-D shapes into realistic 3-D objects with new 3-D effects, such as changing the lighting perspective of a 3-D object.

Perspective shadows – allow you to select from a wide range of shadows with perspective, and you can adjust the depth and angle of each shadow to make pictures more realistic.

Connectors – used to create diagrams and flowcharts with new straight, angled, and curved connectors between the shapes; when shapes are moved, the connectors remain attached and automatically reposition themselves.

Arrowhead styles – allow you to change the width and height of arrowheads for maximum effect.

Object alignment – allows you to distribute and space objects evenly, both horizontally and vertically.

Precise line-width control – allows you increased control over the width of lines by selecting preset options or customised line widths.

Image editing – lets you easily adjust the brightness or contrast of a picture.

Transparent background – allows you to insert a bitmap on your slides or Web pages so as to appear to be part of the design by turning background colours into transparent areas.

Creating a Drawing:

The effects of the drawing tools can be superimposed either on the spreadsheet area or on top of a chart. The result is that you can annotate Excel 97 worksheets or charts to your total satisfaction.

To create an object, click on the required Drawing button, such as the **Oval** or **Rectangle**, position the mouse pointer where you want to create the object on the screen, and then drag the mouse to draw the object. Hold the <Shift> key while you drag the mouse to create a perfect circle or square. If you do not hold <Shift>, Office Art creates an oval or a rectangle.

You can use the **AutoShapes** button to select from a variety of pre-drawn **Lines**, **Basic Shapes**, etc. First click on the desired line or shape, then position the mouse pointer where you want to create the object on the screen and click the left mouse button to fix it on that position.

Editing a Chart:

To select a chart, click on it. Excel displays black handles around the selected chart. You can:

(a) Move an object, or multiple objects, within a draw area of a chart by selecting them and dragging to the desired position. To copy an object, click at the object, then use the **Edit, Copy** / **Edit, Paste** commands. (b) Size an object by positioning the mouse pointer on a black handle and then dragging the handle until the object is the desired shape and size. (c) Delete an object by selecting it and pressing the <Del> key. To delete a drawing, hold the <Shift> key down and click each object in turn that makes up the drawing, unless they are grouped or framed, then press <Del>.

Do try out some of these commands using the **Project 9** Excel file, but do not save the results of your experimentation under the same file name.

5. THE EXCEL DATABASE

An Excel database table is a worksheet range which contains related information, such as 'Customer's Names', 'Consultancy Details', 'Invoice No.', etc. A phone book is a simple database table, stored on paper. In Excel each record is entered as a worksheet row, with the fields of each record occupying corresponding columns.

A database table is a collection of data that exists, and is organised around a specific theme or requirement. It is used for storing information so that it is quickly accessible. To make accessing the data easier, each row (or **record**), of data within a database table is structured in the same fashion, i.e. each record will have the same number of columns (or **fields**).

We define a database and its various elements as follows:

Database table	A collection of related data organised in rows and columns in a worksheet file. A worksheet file can contain many different database tables.
Record	A row of information relating to a single entry and comprising one or more fields.
Field	A single column of information of the same type, such as people's names.

In Excel 97, a database table can contain a maximum of 256 fields and 65,536 records. Furthermore, you can have up to 32,000 characters in a cell, increased from a previous limit of 256 in earlier versions of the package.

Creating a Database

In order to investigate the various database functions, such as sorting, searching, etc., we first need to set up a database table in the form shown on the next page.

Note that in creating a database table, the following rules must be observed:

1. The top row of the database table must contain the field labels, one per column, which identify the fields in the database table. The second and subsequent rows of such a database table must contain records; no blank rows should be inserted between the field labels and the records.

2. Field labels must be unique within a given database table.

3. Entries under each field must be of the same type.

4. The size of a database table must be limited within the design criteria of the package (256 fields and 65,536 records for Excel 97).

We assume that the 'Invoice Analysis' of Adept Consultants is designed and set out as shown below with the listed field titles and field widths.

Column	Title	Width	Type
A	NAME	21	General or Text
B	DETAILS	20	General or Text
C	No.	6	Number, 0 decimals
D	ISSUED	9	Custom, dd/mm/yy
E	PAID?	7	General or Text
F	VALUE	8	Currency, 2 decimals

These widths were chosen so that the whole worksheet could be seen on the screen at once.

If you cannot see all the rows of this database on your screen at once (it depends on the configuration of your display under Windows 95 - see below), either select the **View, Zoom** command and set the zoom level to say 90%, or toggle off the **Drawing** and/or **Status Toolbars**.

If, on the other hand, you did not want to change your Excel configuration, but prefer to change the configuration of your display, then click the **Start** button and select **Settings, Control Panel**, double-click the Display icon and click the Setting tab of the Display Properties dialogue box. In our case, the **Desktop area** was set to 800 by 600 pixels and the **Font size** to Small. However, do remember that if you carry out these changes, they will not take effect until you restart Windows.

	A	B	C	D	E	F	G
1		INVOICE ANALYSIS: ADEPT CONSULTANTS LTD AT					23/09/97
2							
3	NAME	DETAILS	No.	ISSUED	PAID?	VALUE	
4	VORTEX Co. Ltd	Wind Tunnel Tests	97001	10/04/97	N	£120.84	
5	AVON Construction	Adhesive Tests	97002	14/04/97	Y	£103.52	
6	BARROWS Associates	Tunnel Design Tests	97003	20/04/97	N	£99.32	
7	STONEAGE Ltd	Carbon Dating Tests	97004	05/05/97	N	£55.98	
8	PARKWAY Gravel	Material Size Tests (XX)	97005	11/05/97	N	£180.22	
9	WESTWOOD Ltd	Load Bearing Tests	97006	25/05/97	N	£68.52	
10	GLOWORM Ltd	Luminescence Tests	97007	10/06/97	N	£111.55	
11	SILVERSMITH Co	X-Ray Diffraction Test	97008	20/06/97	Y	£123.45	
12	WORMGLAZE Ltd	Heat Transfer Tests	97009	30/06/97	N	£35.87	
13	EALING Engines Design	Vibration Tests	97010	05/07/97	N	£58.95	
14	HIRE Service Equipment	Network Implementation	97011	15/07/97	N	£290.00	
15	EUROBASE Co. Ltd	Project Control	97012	22/07/97	N	£150.00	
16	FREEMARKET Dealers	Stock Control Package	97013	03/08/97	N	£560.00	
17	OILRIG Construct.	Metal Fatigue Tests	97014	12/08/97	N	£96.63	
18	TIME & Motion Ltd	Systems Analysis	97015	26/08/97	N	£120.35	
19	AVON Construction	Cement Fatigue Tests	97016	07/09/97	N	£111.89	
20	PARKWAY Gravel	Material Size Tests (ZZ)	97017	15/09/97	N	£190.35	

To change the width of the various columns to those given on the previous page, use the **Format, Column, Width** command (or use the mouse to drag the vertical separators of the column borders). Next, enter the abbreviated titles, centrally positioned, in row 3, as shown in the worksheet above.

The formatting type was selected by using the **Format, Cells** command to display the dialogue box below.

This dialogue box was used to format column C to a **Number** category format (with 0 decimal places), column D to a **Custom** category format (type dd/mm/yy), and column F to a **Currency** format (with 2 decimal places).

Finally, enter the numeric information in your worksheet and save the worksheet under the filename **Invoice 1**. You could format your database further by choosing a design from a list in the AutoFormat

dialogue box, as shown here, prior to saving your work. However, we leave this to you, as it is entirely a matter of personal choice.

Sorting a Database List:

The records within our database list are in the order in which they were entered, with the 'Invoice No' shown in ascending order. However, we might find it easier to browse through the information if it was sorted in alphabetical order of 'Customer's Name'. Excel has an easy way to do this.

To use it, highlight the database list (data range A4:F20; don't include the field names in the range to be sorted) and, either press the 'Sort Ascending' button, shown here, or select the

Data, Sort

command, and choose in the **Sort By** list of the Sort dialogue box the name of the field on which you want to sort the database (in this case NAME). This will be the primary sort key.

The second method of sorting allows you more control over the sorting options, such as the choice of a secondary sort key (in this case No.). This is selected in the **Then by** list of the Sort dialogue box, shown above, which ensures that the lowest number invoices appear first, if a company has been issued with more than one invoice. You even have the choice of a third sort key, if you needed one.

Pressing the **OK** button produces the display shown on the next page.

The easiest way to return the database to its original sort order is by selecting the **Edit, Undo Sort** command or you can re-sort the database in ascending order of Invoice No.

File Edit View Insert Format Tools Data Window Help

Arial — 10 — **B** *I* U ... AVON Construction

A4 ... AVON Construction

	A	B	C	D	E	F	G	H
1		INVOICE ANALYSIS: ADEPT CONSULTANTS LTD AT					23/09/97	
2								
3	NAME	DETAILS	No.	ISSUED	PAID?	VALUE		
4	AVON Construction	Adhesive Tests	97002	14/04/97	Y	£103.54		
5	AVON Construction	Cement Fatigue Tests	97016	07/09/97	N	£111.89		
6	BARROWS Associates	Tunnel Design Tests	97003	20/04/97	N	£99.32		
7	EALING Engines Design	Vibration Tests	97010	05/07/97	N	£58.95		
8	EUROBASE Co. Ltd	Project Control	97012	22/07/97	N	£150.00		
9	FREEMARKET Dealers	Stock Control Package	97013	03/08/97	N	£560.00		
10	GLOWORM Ltd	Luminescence Tests	97007	10/06/97	N	£111.56		
11	HIRE Service Equipment	Network Implementation	97011	15/07/97	N	£290.00		
12	OILRIG Construct.	Metal Fatigue Tests	97014	12/08/97	N	£96.63		
13	PARKWAY Gravel	Material Size Tests (XX)	97005	11/05/97	N	£180.22		
14	PARKWAY Gravel	Material Size Tests (ZZ)	97017	15/09/97	N	£190.35		
15	SILVERSMITH Co	X-Ray Diffraction Test	97008	20/06/97	Y	£123.45		
16	STONEAGE Ltd	Carbon Dating Tests	97004	05/05/97	N	£55.98		
17	TIME & Motion Ltd	Systems Analysis	97015	26/08/97	N	£120.35		
18	VORTEX Co. Ltd	Wind Tunnel Tests	97001	10/04/97	N	£120.84		
19	WESTWOOD Ltd	Load Bearing Tests	97006	25/05/97	N	£68.52		
20	WORMGLAZE Ltd	Heat Transfer Tests	97009	30/06/97	N	£35.87		

Date Arithmetic

There are several date functions which can be used in Excel 97 to carry out date calculations. For example, typing the function =DATE(97,9,23) or the function =DATEVALUE("23/9/97"), returns the date 23/9/97 provided the cell is formatted as General. If the cell was formatted as Number, then Excel 97 (as with Lotus 1-2-3) would return the number of days since 1 January 1900.

Typing the function =NOW( ), returns the current date and time as given by your computer's internal clock, provided the cell is formatted as General. If the cell was formatted as Number, then Excel returns a decimal number representing the number of days since 1 January 1900, with the digits after the decimal point representing a fraction of a day.

With Excel 97 you don't need to use the DATE and DATEVALUE functions when entering dates. You could, for example, write in a cell the formula:

```
=NOW()-D4
```

which allows Excel 97 to calculate the difference in days between now and the mentioned date.

We could use this formula to work out the number of overdue days of the unpaid invoices in our example, by typing it in cell G4. However, if you want to compare the numbers you get with those displayed in this book, use instead the following formula:

```
=$G$1-D4
```

where $G$1 causes an 'absolute' reference to be made to the contents of cell G1. If the record in row 4 of the worksheet refers to the data of VORTEX Co. Ltd., then the result should be 166 days, provided you are doing this after midday, otherwise it will be 165.

However, before we proceed to copy the above formula to the rest of the G column of the database list, we should take into consideration the fact that, normally, such information is not necessary if an invoice has been paid. Therefore, we need to edit the above formula in such a way as to make the result conditional to non-payment of the issued invoice.

The IF Function

The IF function allows comparison between two values with the use of special 'logical' operators. The logical operators we can use are listed below.

Logical	*operators*
=	Equal to
<	Less than
>	Greater than
<=	Less than or Equal to
>=	Greater than or Equal to
<>	Not Equal to

The general format of the IF function is as follows:

IF(Comparison,Outcome-if-true,Outcome-if-false)

which contains three arguments separated by commas. The first argument of the IF function is the 'logical comparison', the second is what should happen if the outcome of the logical comparison is 'true', while the third is what should happen if the outcome of the logical comparison is 'false'.

Thus, we can incorporate the IF function in the formula we entered in cell G4 to calculate the days overdue only if the invoice has not been paid, otherwise the string 'N/A' should be written into the appropriate cell, should the contents of the corresponding E column of a record be anything else but N. Either edit the formula in cell G4, by double-clicking the cell, or retype it. The final version of the formula in cell G4 should now correspond to:

=IF(E4="N",$G$1–D4," N/A")

Now copy this formula to the rest of the appropriate range (G5:G20) and compare your results with those shown below.

	A	B	C	D	E	F	G
1	⇩	INVOICE ANALYSIS: ADEPT CONSULTANTS LTD AT					23/09/97
2							
3	NAME	DETAILS	No.	ISSUED	PAID?	VALUE	OVERDUE
4	VORTEX Co. Ltd	Wind Tunnel Tests	97001	10/04/97	N	£120.84	166
5	AVON Construction	Adhesive Tests	97002	14/04/97	Y	£103.52	N/A
6	BARROWS Associates	Tunnel Design Tests	97003	20/04/97	N	£99.32	156
7	STONEAGE Ltd	Carbon Dating Tests	97004	05/05/97	N	£55.98	141
8	PARKWAY Gravel	Material Size Tests (XX)	97005	11/05/97	N	£180.22	135
9	WESTWOOD Ltd	Load Bearing Tests	97006	25/05/97	N	£68.52	121
10	GLOWORM Ltd	Luminescence Tests	97007	10/06/97	N	£111.55	105
11	SILVERSMITH Co	X-Ray Diffraction Test	97008	20/06/97	Y	£123.45	N/A
12	WORMGLAZE Ltd	Heat Transfer Tests	97009	30/06/97	N	£35.87	85
13	EALING Engines Design	Vibration Tests	97010	05/07/97	N	£58.95	80
14	HIRE Service Equipment	Network Implementation	97011	15/07/97	N	£290.00	70
15	EUROBASE Co. Ltd	Project Control	97012	22/07/97	N	£150.00	63
16	FREEMARKET Dealers	Stock Control Package	97013	03/08/97	N	£560.00	51
17	OILRIG Construct.	Metal Fatigue Tests	97014	12/08/97	N	£96.63	42
18	TIME & Motion Ltd	Systems Analysis	97015	26/08/97	N	£120.35	28
19	AVON Construction	Cement Fatigue Tests	97016	07/09/97	N	£111.89	16
20	PARKWAY Gravel	Material Size Tests (ZZ)	97017	15/09/97	N	£190.35	8

Your results might differ from the ones shown above, if you have used the NOW( ) function in cell G1. Check your work, then save it under the filename **Invoice 2**.

Searching a Database

A database can be searched for specific records that meet certain criteria. We will use the database of worksheet **Invoice 2** to illustrate the method.

Assuming that the database is on your screen, we need only place the cell pointer within the data list (we put it on cell A4, although anywhere within the range A4:G20 would do), for Excel to instinctively know the range of your data.

Using the Database Form:

After the cell pointer is placed within the database list, Excel creates automatically a database form, as shown below, which is accessed by selecting the **Data, Form** command. The database form can be used to add, delete, edit, and search for specific records.

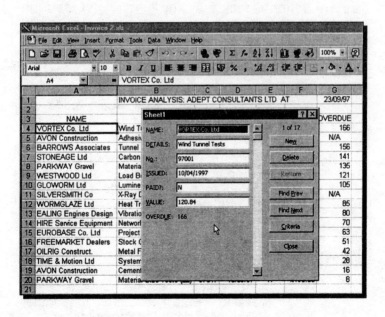

Note that the field names at the top row of the database appear on the left side of the form. On the top right corner of the form (above the **New** button) the entry '1 of 17' is displayed to indicate that this is the first of 17 records.

Most of the field names within the database form have one letter underlined, which can be used to access the corresponding box in the middle of the form in which the value of each field of the particular record is shown. To select fields or buttons, press the <Alt> key plus the underlined letter on field text or button, or point and click with the mouse. To move the highlighter forward through fields and buttons press the <Tab> key, while to move backwards, press <Shift+Tab>.

With the help of the database form, adding new records is made easy. On pressing the **New** button, an empty form. is displayed for you to fill in. Editing a displayed record is even easier; that is why the **Restore** button is included. The functions of the form buttons are as follows:

Button	*Function*
New	Clears the field entries in the displayed form so that new information can be added. Pressing **New** again, adds the data just typed as a new record in the database.
Delete	Deletes the displayed record and shifts the remaining records one up the list. A deleted record cannot be restored. If you delete a record accidentally, re-open the database file without saving the changes.
Restore	Restores edited fields in the displayed record, removing the changes just made. Entries must be restored before pressing <Enter> to scroll to another record, or clicking the **Close** button.

Find Prev	Displays the previous record in the list. If criteria have been selected, then pressing **Find Prev** displays the previous record that matches the criteria.
Find Next	Displays the next record in the list. If criteria have been selected, then pressing **Find Next** displays the next record that matches the criteria.
Criteria	Displays a dialogue box in which you can enter comparison criteria with comparison operators to find records that meet these restrictions.
Close	Closes the data form.
Clear	Available after pressing the **Criteria** button. It removes existing criteria from the Criteria dialogue box.
Form	Available after pressing the **Criteria** button. It returns you to the default data form.

Finding Records:

There are two ways of finding specific records from within a database. The first method involves the use of the database form, while the second method involves the filtering of data by using a criteria range within the worksheet to display only the rows that meet all the specified criteria.

Excel's database form can be used to find records provided the records we are looking for meet simple criteria. To enter the criteria, press the **Criteria** button on the database form which will cause a blank form to be displayed, with the cursor blinking in the first field. Now move to the 'PAID?' field and type N, then to the 'VALUE' field and type >150, as shown on the next page.

On pressing the **Find Next** button, the first record that meets both these criteria is displayed - in this case, the 5th record (PARKWAY Gravel). Pressing the **Find Next** button again three more times, displays the 11th, 13th and 17th record in succession.

To use Excel's second method for finding and extracting data, we need to specify an area of the worksheet for setting our criteria for the search. To do this, first copy the field names of the database (A3:G3) to an empty area of the worksheet, say, A23:G23 which will form the first line of the 'criteria range'. Label this area CRITERIA FOR SEARCHING in cell A22.

Now type in cells E24 and F24 the actual criteria which is N and >150, respectively, then use the **Data, Filter, Advanced Filter** command and specify in the displayed dialogue box the **List Range** and **Criteria Range** as A3:G20 and A23:G24 (it includes the field names in both cases). On pressing the **OK** button, Excel filters the data **in-place** by hiding the rows that do not meet the criteria, as shown below.

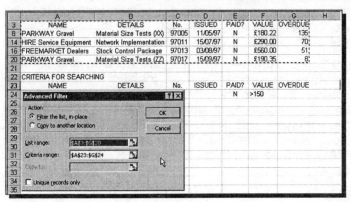

Do not specify an empty line as part of the criterion range, as this has the effect of searching the database for **all** records. The criteria must be entered in the second and subsequent rows of the criterion range, with each entered below the copy of the appropriate field name. A label (text) or a value may be entered exactly as it appears in the database.

In the case of searching a database for label (text), such as under the fields 'NAME' and 'DETAILS' in our example, you can use the two special characters ? and * (known as 'wildcard characters') to match any single character of a label or all characters to the end of the label.

To search a database for values, either enter the value as the exact criterion or use a simple numeric comparison, such as >90, in which the logical operators (<, <=, >, >=, <>) can be used. The logical formula generates a value of 1 if the condition is TRUE or a value of 0 if the condition is FALSE.

Several criteria can be entered, either in the same row, if you want Excel to search for records that match every criterion (i.e. criteria entered are linked with the logical AND), or one per row, if you want Excel to search records that satisfy any of the criteria (i.e. criteria entered are linked with the logical OR).

As seen above, selecting the **Filter the list, in-place** option in the Advanced Filter dialogue box, causes Excel to hide the rows that do not meet the specified criteria. To see the full database list again, use the **Data, Filter, Show All** command.

Extracting Records

To extract records and have them copied into another area of the worksheet, we need to select the **Copy to another location** option in the Advanced Filter dialogue box. But first, we need to set up a second area - the 'output range'. To do this, copy the field names to the cell range A28:G28 and label it as 'OUTPUT RANGE' in cell A27, as shown below.

Note that we chose to put the criteria and output ranges in rows below the actual database (perhaps not the best position), rather than on the side of it. This avoids the errors that might ensue should we later decide to insert a row in our database, which will also insert a row in the criteria/output range. For a more structured worksheet layout, see end of chapter.

Save this worksheet under the filename **Invoice 3**.

Structuring a Workbook

In a well designed workbook, areas of calculations using formulae should be kept on a separate sheet from the data entry sheet. The reason for this is to prevent accidental overwriting of formulae that might be contained within the data entry sheet.

As an example, we will use the **Invoice 3** file, but instead of extracting data into the same sheet, we will use another sheet into which to copy the extracted records. To do this, first open file **Invoice 3**, then use the **Window, New Window** command, followed by the **Window, Arrange** command and click the **Horizontal** radio button on the displayed dialogue box. Next, activate the lower window and click on the Sheet2 tab to display an empty worksheet at the bottom half of the screen, as shown below.

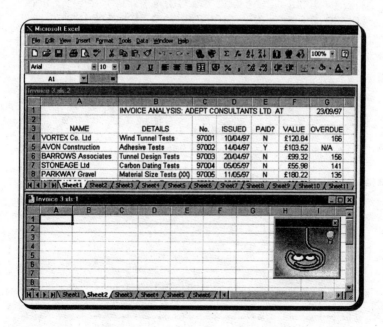

Now use the **Edit, Cut** and **Edit, Paste** commands to transfer cell range A22:G28 of Sheet1 to a range starting at cell A1 of Sheet2 and adjust the widths of the various columns to match those of Sheet1 (also, don't forget to delete from Sheet1 any extracted data from a previous search).

Note: Excel only extracts data into an active sheet. Therefore, you must make Sheet2 the active sheet, and since the program also requires to know which are the database field labels, place the cell pointer in cell A7, before you use the **Data, Filter, Advanced Filter** command. The address in the **List range** box of the Advanced Filter dialogue box must be specified (you can either type it in or use the buttons to the right of the entry box to point to the required range) to indicate the correct address for the database list which is

```
Sheet1!$A$3:$G$20
```

The **Criteria range** and the **Copy to** address locations should be similarly prefixed with Sheet2! for correct data extraction. To access the entry box of the latter, click the **Copy to another location** radio button on the Advanced Filter dialogue box, as shown below.

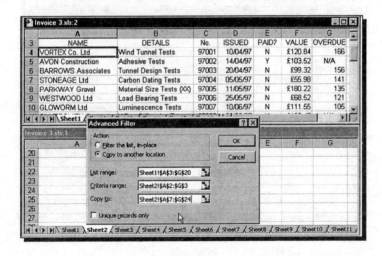

Pressing the **OK** button causes the records that match the specified criteria to be extracted from Sheet1 and copied into Sheet2, as shown below.

	A	B	C	D	E	F	G
6	OUTPUT RANGE						
7	NAME	DETAILS	No.	ISSUED	PAID?	VALUE	OVERDUE
8	PARKWAY Gravel	Material Size Tests (XX)	97005	11/05/97	N	£180.22	135
9	HIRE Service Equipment	Network Implementation	97011	15/07/97	N	£290.00	70
10	FREEMARKET Dealers	Stock Control Package	97013	03/08/97	N	£560.00	51
11	PARKWAY Gravel	Material Size Tests (ZZ)	97017	15/09/97	N	£190.35	8
12							
13							

Save the resultant workbook under the filename **Invoice 4**.

Another aspect of structuring, is the provision of a screen with technical information about the contents of the particular workbook; a kind of an overview of the function of the worksheet application. This area should also contain instructions for the use of the particular application at hand. Such information can help you in the future, or help others to learn and use an application easily and effectively. If you use range names, then include a range name table in your information screen(s).

Finally, provide a separate sheet within a workbook, or a separate worksheet altogether, for macros (the subject of Chapter 8), which are in a programming language that allows you to chain together menu commands. Sensitive sheets or indeed whole workbooks can be protected using the **Tools, Protection** command and either select the **Protect Sheet** or the **Protect Workbook** option, according to your application needs, to restrict cell entries to unprotected cells. This prevents accidental changes being made to cells containing formulae.

A good spreadsheet design, using the 3-dimensional ability of Excel 97 could be as follows:

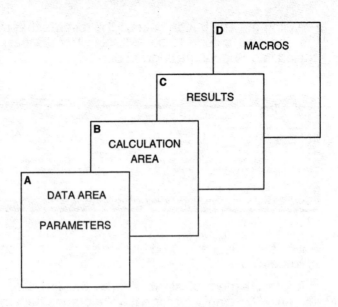

Obviously, the headings of the various workbook sheets above could be different. They would largely depend on the application at hand.

6. OTHER TOOLS AND CAPABILITIES

As well as the **Spelling** and **AutoCorrect** tools, to be found under the **Tools** menu option, Excel 97 comes with an integrated Auditor, and tools to solve what-if type of problems such as the Goal Seek, What-if Tables, Solver and Scenarios. A short description of each of these is given below.

The Auditor

You use the Auditor to analyse the way your worksheet is structured, or for locating the source of errors in formulae.

When you invoke the Auditor by selecting the **Tools, Auditing** command, the options sub-menu is displayed, as shown below.

In this you can specify what you want to audit on the current file (for a description of the options see below), the default being **Trace Precedents**.

The Audit options have the following functions:

Option	Function
Trace precedents	Identifies all cells in the audit file that provide data for a particular formula.
Trace dependents	Identifies all formulae in the audit file that refer to a particular cell.
Trace Error	Identifies all cells involved in the production of an error, such as a circular reference.

Remove All Arrows	Removes the identifying arrows placed on the worksheet as a result of invoking the previous options.
Show Auditing Toolbar	Toggles the display of the Auditing Toolbar on and off.

As an example, we show below an audit on the file **Project 3**, for the first two options. For the first option, select cell E9, then use the **Tools, Auditing, Trace Precedents** command, while for the second option, select cell B11, then use the **Tools, Auditing, Trace Dependents** command.

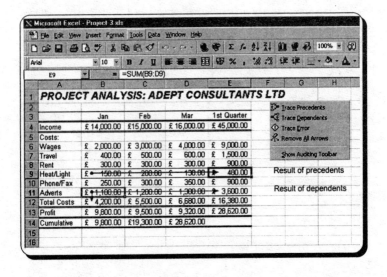

To remove the arrows resulting from the above choice of auditing options, use the **Tools, Remove All Arrows** command.

Save the file under the filename **Tools 1**, as we will be using it to illustrate the next Excel 97 Tool.

The Goal Seek

You use the **Goal Seek** to fine-tune a formula that gives you the required result by changing one of the variables that affect the final value. As an example, we will use the information in the **Tools 1** file. If you don't have this file, use the **Project 3** file and save it as **Tools 1**.

To effectively use Goal Seek, you must adhere to the following procedure:

- Type the formula to be fine-tuned by Goal Seek in a cell. We will use the **=sum(B4:D4)** formula in cell E4 of our example.

- Invoke Goal Seek, by using the **Tools, Goal Seek** command which displays the Goal Seek dialogue box shown below.

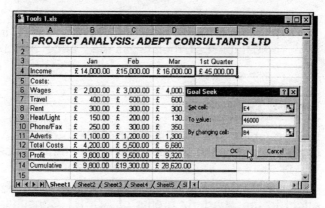

In this dialogue box you can specify in the **Set cell** box the address or range name of the cell that contains the formula you want to fine-tune, as shown above. In the **To value** box you type the value you want the formula in the formula cell to equate to when Goal Seek solves the problem, while in the **By changing cell** box the address of the cell whose value Goal Seek can change.

- Click the **OK** button to find an answer to the problem, displayed below (it changed the contents of B4 from £14,000 to £15,000). If it can't be done, you will be told.

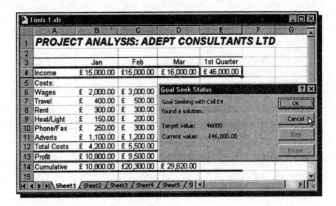

If you don't want to lose the original values in the adjustable cell, then press the **Cancel** button.

What-if Tables

What-if tables are used if you require to calculate and display the results of substituting different values for one or more (up to three) variables in a formula.

For example, suppose we wanted to examine the effect to the quarterly profits of ADEPT Consultants if we varied the quarterly income from £35,000 to £55,000, in steps of £5,000. This problem is, of course, rather trivial, but suppose at the same time we expected a wage award increase of between 0% to 3%, while all other costs were tied to inflation which could change from 3% to 5%. This becomes rather more difficult to analyse. However, using what-if tables reduces the problem to something more manageable.

A Two-Input What-if Table:

To illustrate the above problem, but simplifying it by forgetting inflation, we will use the **Tools 1** file (you could use **Project 3** instead). Use the **Window, Freeze Panes** command, then fill in the range F2:K9, as shown below:

Note: A two-input what-if table has two input cells - in our example these are: Input 1 in cell G2 (which refers to the rows) and input 2 in cell G3 (which refers to the columns), representing 'Wage increases' and 'Income', respectively. The value in each of these cells is the first value in their respective ranges, which are F6:F9 and G5:K5. Thus, income varies from £35,000 to £55,000, while wage increases vary from 0% to 3%. Finally, a formula is required in cell F5 which represents profits and which refers to the two input cells defined above. The formula used is:

```
=G3-(E6*(1+G2)+SUM(E7:E11))
```

To verify that this formula is correct, change the input in the 'Income' cell (G3) to £45,000, which should give you the same profit in cell F5 as that shown in cell E13.

The formula in a two-input what-if table must be placed in the top-left corner of the table. Which cell is declared as a 'row input' and a 'column input' in the Table dialogue box is very important. In the case of a one-input what-if table, Excel expects the input range to be either in one column, with the formula placed at the top of the next column to the right of the input column, or in one row, with the formula placed at the top of the next row to the left of the input row.

Before proceeding with the analysis of our problem, save your work under the filename **Tools 2**, then select the effective table range F5:K9 by highlighting it. Next, use the **Data, Table** command and enter G3 in the **Row Input cell** box of the displayed dialogue box, and G2 in the **Column Input Cell** box, as shown below:

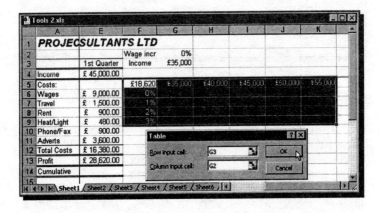

Selecting the **OK** button, displays the results shown on the next page, which you could save under the filename **Tools 3**.

	A	E	F	G	H	I	J	K
1	**PROJECSULTANTS LTD**							
2			Wage incr	0%				
3		1st Quarter	Income	£35,000				
4	Income	£ 45,000.00						
5	Costs:		£18,620	£35,000	£40,000	£45,000	£50,000	£55,000
6	Wages	£ 9,000.00	0%	18620	23620	28620	33620	38620
7	Travel	£ 1,500.00	1%	18530	23530	28530	33530	38530
8	Rent	£ 900.00	2%	18440	23440	28440	33440	38440
9	Heat/Light	£ 480.00	3%	18350	23350	28350	33350	38350
10	Phone/Fax	£ 900.00						
11	Adverts	£ 3,600.00						
12	Total Costs	£ 16,380.00						
13	Profit	£ 28,620.00						
14	Cumulative							

Tools 2.xls

Sheet1 / Sheet2 / Sheet3 / Sheet4 / Sheet5 / Sheet6

Editing a Data Table:

The input values and formula in the top leftmost column of a data table can be edited at any time. However, the actual results calculated within the data table cannot be edited individually, because they are an array. Some editing operations require you to select the entire data table, while others require you to select only the resulting values. For example:

- To clear the resulting values from a data table, select the resulting values only (G6:G9 in our example) and press the <Del> key. Individual resulting values cannot be cleared separately.

- To copy resulting values from a data table, select them and use the **Edit, Copy** command. Doing this results in copying the values only, not the formulae for those values. Subsequent use of the **Paste Special** command converts the resulting values array into a range of constant values.

- To move, delete, or modify a table, first select the entire data table (F5:K9 in our example). If you are moving the table, having selected it, then click the border of the selection and drag it to a new location on your worksheet.

The Solver

You use the Solver if you want to analyse data in a worksheet and solve 'what-if' type of problems. Solver is ideal for problems that have more than one answer. It can investigate different options and present you with alternative solutions, including the best match to your requirements.

To use Solver, you start with a worksheet model. Solver problems can be set up in one or more worksheet files in memory, by selecting which cells to adjust, adding logical formulae, and defining the limits of the required answers.

As an example, let us analyse more closely ADEPT Consultants' 1st Quarter results. We use the information held in Sheet1 of the **Tools 1** file (you could use the **Project 3** file instead). On a Sheet other than Sheet1 of either file, we add the following information and save the resultant workbook under the filename **Tools 4**.

	A	B	C	D	E	F	G	H
2								
3		Type	Home	Abroad	Total			
4								
5	Number		30	20				
6	Income/consultancy		666.6666	1250				
7	Hours/consultancy		60	160				
8	Costs/consultancy		213.3333	500				
9								
10	Total Income		20000	25000	45000			
11	Total Costs		6400	10000	16400			
12	Total Hours		1800	3200	5000			
13	Total Profit		13600	15000	28600			
14								
15	Constraints							
16	Maximum hours available<=6000							
17	Minimum Home Consultancies >=25							
18	Minimum Abroad Consultancies >=15							
19	Minimum Profit >=28600							
20								

Sheet1 \ **Sheet2** \ Sheet3 \ Sheet4 \ Sheet5 \

What we assume here is that ADEPT Consultants operate both at home and abroad. In the first quarter they undertook 30 consultancies at home and 20 consultancies abroad.

The range C5:D8 holds numerical information on the income, hours taken, and the costs per consultancy, respectively.

In range C10:D13 we have entered formulae to calculate the total income, costs, hours spent, and profit made from each type of consultancy from information held in range C5:D8, while range E10:E13 summates the two types of consultancies.

Cells E12 and E13 hold the total time spent in consultancies and the total profit made, respectively, which is very important information.

What we would like to do now is to increase the consultancies to make up the maximum available time in the three month period, which is 6000 hours, while maximising the profit. The question is 'what mixture of consultancies (home or abroad) is more profitable?'

Starting the Solver:

To start Solver use the **Tools, Solver** command, which displays the following Solver Parameters dialogue box:

Next, we would like to enter the constraints under which we will impose a solution to our problem. These can be added, changed or deleted with the use of the three buttons at the bottom of the Solver Parameters dialogue box shown above.

Entering Constraints:

At the bottom of the worksheet, we have included certain constraints, discussed below, which are entered as logical formulae in the range E16:E19 using the Add Constraint dialogue box, shown here, by clicking the **Add** button on the Solver Parameters dialogue box.

 After entering each one of these, press the **Add** button so that you can enter the next one.

The logic behind these constraints is as follows:

- Since the maximum available hours in a quarter must remain less than or equal to 6000 hours, we enter in cell E16 the formula **E12<=6000**.

- Since a long term contract with the government requires that at least 25 consultancies are undertaken at home, we enter in cell E17 the formula **C5>=25**.

- Since a similar long term contract with a foreign government requires that at least 15 consultancies are undertaken abroad, we enter in cell E18 the formula **D5>=15**.

- Since we would like to maximise profits, we enter in cell E19 the formula **E13>=28600**.

Solving a Problem:

Once the last constraint is inserted into the Add Constraint dialogue box, pressing the **OK** button causes the return of the Solver Preferences box.

Next, specify the **Set Target Cell**, as E13, then the adjustable cells in the **By Changing Cells** box as C5:D5 - these are cells that contain values that Solver can adjust when it searches for an answer.

Finally, press the **Solve** button which causes Solver to find a solution, place the answer in the worksheet and display the Solver Results dialogue box, as shown below.

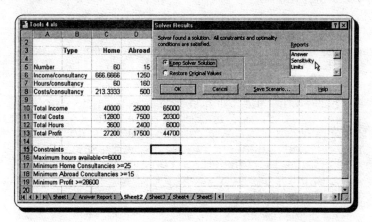

You now have a choice of either keeping the values found by Solver, or reverting to the original worksheet values. Also from the **Reports** section of the dialogue box you can choose to display one of three report types: Answer, Sensitivity, and Limits. Selecting one of these causes Excel to produce an appropriate report and place it in a separate Sheet. Finally, restore the original values and save your work as **Tools 5**.

If a problem is too complex for the default settings of Solver, then click at the **Options** button on the Solver Parameters dialogue box to display the Solver Options dialogue box, in which you can change the time limit for solving a problem, the maximum iterations allowed, and even select the type of model to be used.

Managing What-if Scenarios

There are times when we would like to examine different what-if scenarios created from a single spreadsheet model. Normally, managers tend to copy the model to different parts of the spreadsheet so as to examine and display different assumptions. However, keeping track of all the different assumptions can become extremely problematic, mostly confusing, and indeed wasteful of spreadsheet space and, therefore, computer memory.

With Excel you can use the Scenario Manager to keep all the different versions of the same worksheet model together. In addition, you can also give each version a meaningful name, such as 'Original Case', 'Best Case', and 'Worst Case'.

To illustrate the method, we will use the **Tools 5** example which we employed when discussing the Solver. In addition, we assume that it is possible to reduce the number of hours it takes ADEPT Consultants to complete a consultancy at home or abroad, but if one is reduced the other is increased by the same amount.

The model looks as shown on the next page, with '% Changes' added in columns F and G, the contents of cells C7 and D7 changed to =60*(1+F7) and =160*(1+G7), respectively, and the overall profit now also displayed in column H, by inserting in H5 the reference =E13. Obviously, since we will be optimising our solutions, you must learn to use Solver first.

Finally, save your model as **Tools 6** before running it. This ensures that you can go back to it if anything goes wrong.

Next, enter 0% change on the hours per consultancy on both the home and abroad input cells, then run the Solver for an optimum answer on profits using the already defined constraints. This gives us a profit of £44,700, which is in fact our no change scenario.

110

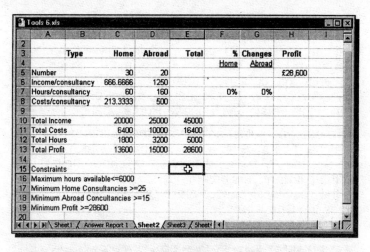

Next, click the **Save Scenario** button on the Solver Results dialogue box to activate the Scenario Manager which displays the Save Scenario dialogue box, as shown below.

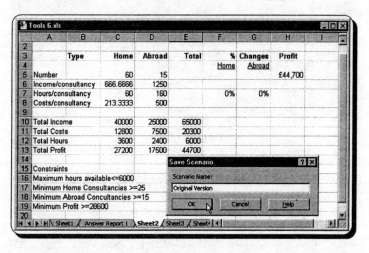

Now add the description 'Original Version' and press the **OK** button, which returns you to the Solver Results dialogue box and press the **OK** button to 'Keep the Solver Solution'.

Next, change the contents of cells F7 and G7 to –5% and 5%, respectively, and activate the Solver for an optimum answer on profits, saving the scenario as 'Negative Home Change'. Once more, change the contents of cells F7 and G7 to 5% and –5%, respectively, and then repeat the above procedure, but saving this version as 'Positive Home Change'.

To see and select any one of the defined scenarios, use the **Tools, Scenarios** command which displays the Scenario Manager dialogue box, shown below, with all the different versions of our solutions listed. To look at the results of one of these, simply highlight it and press the **Show** button.

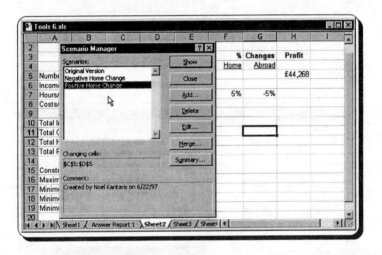

Last but not least, Scenario Manager allows you to merge several versions together and define them as a scenario, and create a summary report - you have a choice of two. The first report is a 'scenario summary', while the second is a 'scenario pivot table'. With the pivot table you get an instant what-if analysis of different scenario combinations.

Finally, if you intend to work with scenarios, save your work as **Tools 7**.

7. SHARING INFORMATION

You can link or embed all or part of an existing file created either in an Office application or in any other application that supports Object Linking and Embedding (OLE). However, if an application does not support OLE, then you must use the copy/cut and paste commands to copy or move information from one application to another.

In general, you copy, move, link or embed information depending on the imposed situation, as follows:

Imposed Situation	*Method to Adopt*
Inserted information will not need updating, or Application does not support OLE.	Copy or move
Inserted information needs to be auto-matically updated in the destination file as changes are made to the data in the source file, or Source file will always be available and you want to minimise the size of the destination file, or Source file is to be shared amongst several users.	Link
Inserted information might need to be updated but source file might not be always accessible, or Destination files needs to be edited without having these changes reflected in the source file.	Embed
To jump to a location in a worksheet or Web page, or to a file that was created in a different program.	Hyperlink

Copying or Moving Information

To copy or move information between programs running under Windows, such as Microsoft applications, is extremely easy. To move information, use the drag and drop facility, while to copy information, use the **Edit, Copy** and **Edit, Paste** commands.

To illustrate the technique, we will use a file created in Lotus 1-2-3 containing the solution of a 'Compound Interest' problem. We will consider the following two possibilities:

Source File Available without Application:

We assume that you only have the source file **comp_Int.WK4** on disc, but not the application that created it (that is you don't have Lotus 1-2-3). In such a situation, you can only copy the contents of the whole file to the destination (in our case an Excel worksheet). To achieve this, do the following:

- Start Excel and minimise it on the Taskbar.

- Use My Computer (or Explorer) to locate the file whose contents you want to copy into an Excel workbook.

- Click the filename that you want to copy, hold the mouse button down and point to Excel on the Taskbar until the application opens.

- While still holding the mouse button down, move the mouse pointer into Excel's open worksheet to the point where you would like to insert the contents of **comp_int.WK4**.

- Release the mouse button to place the contents of **comp_int.WK4** into Excel at that point.

The result is shown below. As you can see, Excel 97 has preserved the formatting styles contained in the Lotus 1-2-3 file, and also drawn a chart automatically, placing it on a separate sheet.

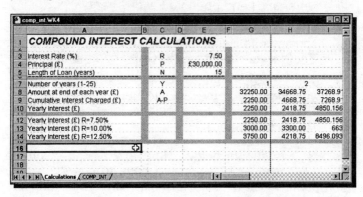

Clicking the COMP_INT sheet, reveals the following:

Source File and Application Available:

Assuming that you have both the file and the application that created it on your computer, you can copy all or part of the contents of the source file to the destination file. Here we also consider two possibilities:

To copy part of a spreadsheet file (in our case part of **comp_int.WK4**) into an Excel workbook, do the following:

- Start your source spreadsheet (whichever you happened to use - in our case it is Lotus 1-2-3 Version 5) and open your worksheet.

- Highlight as much information as you would like to copy into Excel, and click the copy icon on the Toolbar (or use the **Edit, Copy** command).

- Start Excel 97 and place the cell indicator where you would like the data to appear and click the Paste icon on the Toolbar (or use the **Edit, Paste** command).

The result is shown below. Note that all the columns have the same width - you will have to change these appropriately, and the formulae in your original worksheet did not copy across - only the displayed values.

However, normally we tend to want to incorporate part of an Excel worksheet into a word processed document. This document might have been created in Word 97, or any other Windows word processor.

To copy part of an Excel worksheet (say **Project 3**) into a document, do the following:

- Start Excel and open **Project 3**.

- Highlight as much information as you would like to copy and click the copy icon on the Toolbar (or use the **Edit, Copy** command).

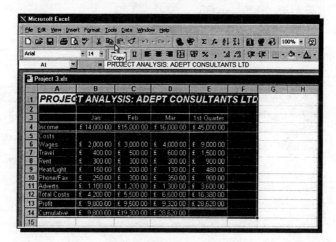

- Start your word processor, place the insertion pointer at the desired place, and click the Paste icon on the Toolbar (or use the **Edit, Paste** command).

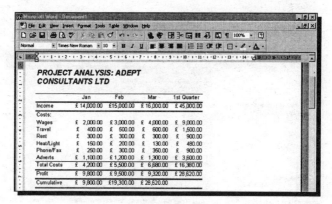

Inserting an Excel Worksheet in Word 97

If the 'Insert Excel Worksheet' button, shown here, appears on your Word 97 Toolbar, you can use it to insert a worksheet of the required number of rows and columns, by simply clicking the button and dragging down to the right. As you drag the mouse, the 'Worksheet' button expands to create the grid of rows and columns, shown below, in a similar manner to that of creating rows and columns of tables.

When you release the mouse button, the worksheet is inserted in your Word document. You can then insert data and apply functions to them. To see which functions are available, click the Paste Function button.

Object Linking and Embedding

Object Linking is copying information from one file (the source file) to another file (the destination file) and maintaining a connection between the two files. When information in the source file is changed, then the information in the destination file is automatically updated. Linked data is stored in the source file, while the file into which you place the data stores only the location of the source and displays a representation of the linked data.

For example, you would use Object Linking if you would want an Excel chart included in, say, a Word document to be updated whenever you changed the information used to create the chart in the first place within Excel. In such a case, the Excel worksheet containing the chart would be referred to as the source file, while the Word document would be referred to as the destination file.

Object Embedding is inserting information created in one file (the source file) into another file (the container file). After such information has been embedded, the object becomes part of the container file. When you double-click an embedded object, it opens in the application in which it was created in the first place. You can then edit it in place, and the original object in the source application remains unchanged.

Thus, the main differences between linking and embedding are where the data is stored and how it is updated after you place it in your file. Linking saves you disc space as only one copy of the linked object is kept on disc. Embedding a logo chosen for your headed paper, saves the logo with every saved letter!

In what follows, we will discuss how you can link or embed either an entire file or selected information from an existing file, and how you can edit an embedded object.

Embedding a New Object:

To embed a new object into an Excel workbook, do the following:

- Open the container file, say **Project 3**, click where you want to embed the new object, and use the **Insert, Object** command. This opens the Object dialogue box, shown below, when the **Create New** tab is clicked.

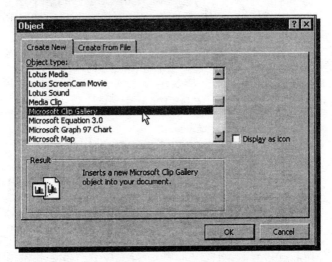

Only applications installed on your PC which support linking and embedding appear in the **Object type** box.

- In the **Object type** box, click the type of object you want to create, and press **OK**.

As an example, we selected Microsoft Clip Gallery (you could select a different application) which opens the Clip Gallery dialogue box, shown on the next page, from which we selected the object shown here from the Currency category. Pressing the **Insert** button on the Clip Gallery dialogue box, embeds the object within the Excel worksheet.

If you were able to follow our suggestions, your worksheet should now look as shown below.

Double-clicking on such an object, opens up the original application. If all is well, save this worksheet under the filename **Share 1**.

Linking or Embedding an Existing File:

To embed an existing, say Word 97, file in its entirety into Excel 97, do the following:

- Open the container file, say **Project 3**, and click where you want to embed the Word file.

- Use the **Insert, Object** command, to open the Object dialogue box, shown below, when the **Create from File** tab is clicked.

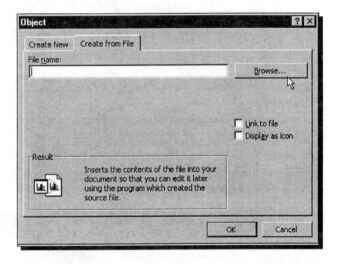

To locate the file you want to link or embed, click **Browse**, and then select the options you want.

- In the **File name** box, type the name of the file you want to link or embed (we used one typed into Word and named **Testdoc.doc**).

- If you wanted to maintain a link to the original file, check the **Link to file** box.

Finally, click the **OK** button to embed your Word file into Excel. The result is shown on the next page.

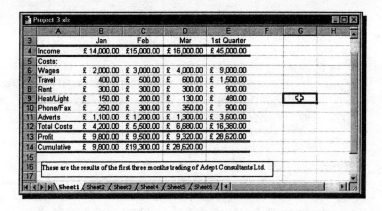

Note: To insert graphics files into an Excel worksheet, use the **Insert, Picture** command instead of the **Insert, Object, From File** command. This opens up the Insert Picture dialogue box which allows you to specify within a **Look in** box the folder and file you want to insert.

As an example, we used below the **Insert, Object** command while **Project 3** was opened, and selected the **Account.bmp** file from Microsoft's Clipart folder.

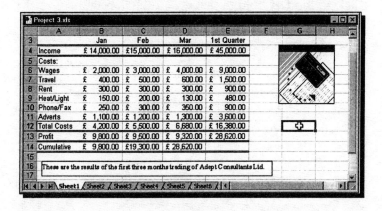

Save this Excel worksheet under the filename **Share 2**.

Editing an Embedded Object:

If the application in which you created an embedded object is installed on your computer, double-click the object to open it for editing. Some applications start the original application in a separate window and then open the object for editing, while other applications temporarily replace the menus and toolbars in the current application so that you can edit the embedded object in place, without switching to another window.

If the application in which you created an embedded object is not installed on your computer, convert the object to the file format of an application you do have. For example, if your word processed document contains an embedded Microsoft Works Spreadsheet object and you do not have Works, you can convert the object to an Excel Workbook format and edit it in Excel.

Some embedded objects, such as sound and video clips, when double-clicked start playing their contents, instead of opening an application for editing. To illustrate this, copy the Goodtime video icon from its folder **Funstuff\Videos** in the Windows 95 CD into Excel using the **Insert, Object** command (click the **Create from File** tab and **Browse** to the required icon. Clicking the **OK** button, displays the following:

	A	B	C	D	E	F	G
Share 3.xls							
1	**PROJECT ANALYSIS: ADEPT CONSULTANTS LTD**						
2							
3		Jan	Feb	Mar	1st Quarter		
4	Income	£ 14,000.00	£15,000.00	£ 16,000.00	£ 45,000.00		
5	Costs:						F:\FUNSTUFF\
6	Wages	£ 2,000.00	£ 3,000.00	£ 4,000.00	£ 9,000.00		IDEOS\GOODTIME.A\
7	Travel	£ 400.00	£ 500.00	£ 600.00	£ 1,500.00		
8	Rent	£ 300.00	£ 300.00	£ 300.00	£ 900.00		
9	Heat/Light	£ 150.00	£ 200.00	£ 130.00	£ 480.00		
10	Phone/Fax	£ 250.00	£ 300.00	£ 350.00	£ 900.00		
11	Adverts	£ 1,100.00	£ 1,200.00	£ 1,300.00	£ 3,600.00		
12	Total Costs	£ 4,200.00	£ 5,500.00	£ 6,680.00	£ 16,380.00		
13	Profit	£ 9,800.00	£ 9,500.00	£ 9,320.00	£ 28,620.00		
14	Cumulative	£ 9,800.00	£19,300.00	£ 28,620.00			
15							

Double-clicking the Goodtime icon, starts the video. To edit the video, select it and use the **Edit, Video Clip Object, Edit** command. Doing this, displays the following:

Of course, unless you have the facilities required for editing videos, you will be unable to do so.

If your embedded object was a sound clip, instead of a video, then the **Video Clip Object** command appearing under the **Edit** menu would change to **Wave Sound Object**. Excel automatically senses the embedded object and changes the menu option appropriately.

Hyperlinks

Excel 97 workbooks and other Office 97 documents can be made more interesting by inserting hyperlinks to other items. A hyperlink causes a jump to another location in the current document or Web page, to a different document or Web page, or to a file that was created in a different program. You can, for example, jump from an Excel workbook to a Word document or to a PowerPoint slide to see more detail.

A hyperlink is represented by a 'hot' image or by display text (which is often blue and underlined) that you click to jump to a different location. To insert a hyperlink into a Workbook, a document, or a Web page, select the display text or image, and either use the **Insert, Hyperlink** command or click the Insert

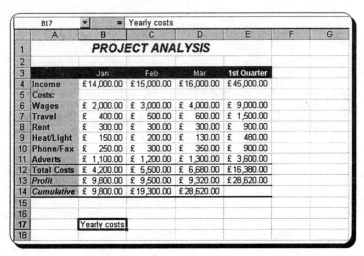

Hyperlink icon on the Toolbar, shown here. Either action opens a dialogue box which allows you to browse for the destination address.

To illustrate the procedure, start Excel, open the **Project 4** file, and type in cell B17 the words 'Yearly costs', as shown below.

	B17	▼	=	Yearly costs			
	A	B	C	D	E	F	G
1			*PROJECT ANALYSIS*				
2							
3		Jan	Feb	Mar	1st Quarter		
4	Income	£ 14,000.00	£ 15,000.00	£ 16,000.00	£ 45,000.00		
5	Costs:						
6	Wages	£ 2,000.00	£ 3,000.00	£ 4,000.00	£ 9,000.00		
7	Travel	£ 400.00	£ 500.00	£ 600.00	£ 1,500.00		
8	Rent	£ 300.00	£ 300.00	£ 300.00	£ 900.00		
9	Heat/Light	£ 150.00	£ 200.00	£ 130.00	£ 480.00		
10	Phone/Fax	£ 250.00	£ 300.00	£ 350.00	£ 900.00		
11	Adverts	£ 1,100.00	£ 1,200.00	£ 1,300.00	£ 3,600.00		
12	Total Costs	£ 4,200.00	£ 5,500.00	£ 6,680.00	£ 16,380.00		
13	*Profit*	£ 9,800.00	£ 9,500.00	£ 9,320.00	£ 28,620.00		
14	*Cumulative*	£ 9,800.00	£ 19,300.00	£ 28,620.00			
15							
16							
17		Yearly costs					
18							

While cell B17 is the active cell, click the Hyperlink icon on the Toolbar and locate the **Project 9** file using the first **Browse** button in the displayed Insert Hyperlink dialogue box. Pressing the **OK** button, inserts the file name in the **Link to file or URL** box, as shown below.

Next, put the insertion pointer in the **Named location in file (optional)** box and click its **Browse** button which displays the second Browse Workbook dialogue box, shown above. In this dialogue box, select the item 'Costs Pie' and delete the contents of the **Reference** box. Pressing the **OK** button of each dialogue box, underlines the text in B17, as shown below, and changes its colour to blue.

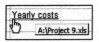

Pointing to such a hyperlink, changes the mouse pointer to a hand, as shown here to the left, and left-clicking it, displays the 'Costs Pie' Sheet of the **Project 9** file. When you have finished looking at the pie chart, click the Back icon on the Toolbar, shown here to the right, for the program to return you automatically to the hyperlinked Excel workbook. If the location of the file you wanted to hyperlink to is incorrect, then errors will obviously occur. Save your work as **Share 4**.

To remove unwanted hyperlinks, place the cell pointer on the hyperlinked cell, click the Insert Hyperlink icon again, and press the **Remove Link** button at the bottom left of the displayed dialogue box.

As a second example, type the words 'Yearly data' in cell D17 in the **Share 4** worksheet and hyperlink this to the 'Consolidation' Sheet of **Project 9**. Doing this allows you to access both the yearly Costs Pie chart and the Consolidation data in the **Project 9** workbook from the **Share 4** worksheet via the hyperlinks. We leave the completion of this exercise to you.

8. USING MACROS

In Excel 97 and other spreadsheet packages, you can automate tasks or create complete applications by writing macros. A macro is simply a set of instructions made up of a sequence of keystrokes, mouse selections, or commands which, in the case of Excel 97 are stored in a Visual Basic module. After saving, or writing, a macro and attaching a quick key combination to it, you can run the same sequence of commands whenever you want. This can save a lot of time and, especially with repetitive operations, can save mistakes creeping into your work.

In Excel there are two basic ways of creating macros. The first one involves the use of Visual Basic, the programming language that is common to all Office 97 applications. With this method, you can write quite complex macro programs directly into a macro file using the Visual Basic Editor which allows you to edit macros, copy macros from one module to another, copy macros between different workbooks, rename the modules that store the macros, or rename the macros. Understanding Visual Basic makes it easier to also program with other Microsoft applications that use the language.

For simple work however, you don't really have to learn to program in Visual Basic, as Excel includes a Macro Recorder which provides you with the second method of generating macros. The Macro Recorder stores the actions you take and the commands you use while working with Excel, which can then be played back (run) to repeat the recorded actions and commands.

Before you record or write a macro, plan the steps and commands you want the macro to perform. This is essential, because if you make a mistake when you record the macro, corrections you make will also be recorded. Each time you record a macro, the macro is stored in a new module attached to a workbook.

Using the Macro Recorder

We will now use the worksheet saved under **Project 3** (see page 46) to show how we can use Excel's Macro Recorder to create a macro to perform 'what-if' type of projections by, say, increasing the 'Wages' bill by 15%.

If you haven't saved **Project 3** on disc, it will be necessary for you to enter the information shown below into Excel so that you can benefit from what is to be introduced at this point.

If you have saved **Project 3**, then use the **File, Open** command to display the worksheet as shown below.

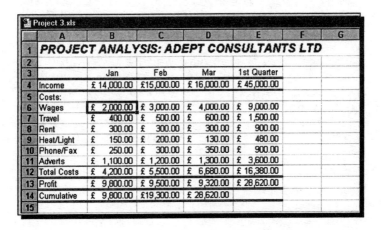

What we would like to do now is to edit the entries under 'Wages' so that this part of the costs can be increased by 15%. One way of doing this would be to multiply the contents of each cell containing the 'wages' value by 1.15.

130

To do this, we would start by changing the contents of cell B6 into a formula, by pressing the F2 function key to 'Edit' the value in it by adding an equals sign at the beginning of the entry and then typing '*1.15' at the end of it, which has the effect of multiplying the contents of the cell by 1.15, thus increasing its contents by 15%. We would then press the <Enter> key which would cause the cell pointer to drop to B7, press the ↑ arrow key to move back to cell B6, then press the → arrow key to move to cell C6 and repeat the whole procedure. The exact steps, after highlighting cell B6, are as follows:

Manual Procedure

Press **F2** to 'Edit' cell
Press the <Home> key to move to beginning of entry
Type = to change entry to formula
Press <End> to move to the end of the entry
Type *1.15
Press the <Enter> key
Press ↑ arrow key
Press → arrow key.

Recording an Excel 97 Macro:

Having opened the **Project 3** file, highlight cell B6 - the first cell we want to operate on. Then, select the **Tools, Macro, Record New Macro** command which displays the Record Macro dialogue box with the default **Macro name** given as Macro1. This can be changed by you to some more meaningful name, if you so wished.

In the Record Macro dialogue box, we specified that the **Shortcut key** should be Ctrl+w (w for wages), as shown on the screen dump on the next page.

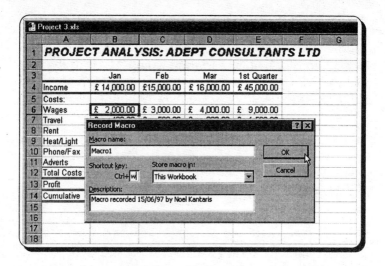

On pressing the **OK** button, Excel displays the Stop Recording button, shown here. Everything you type from now on becomes part of the macro. To start recording our macro, press/type the appropriate key/information, as shown below.

F2
<Home>
=
<End>
*1.15
<Enter>
Press ↑ arrow key
Press → arrow key.

followed by clicking the Stop Recording button shown above (or by choosing the **Tools**, **Record Macros**, **Stop Macros** menu command).

To see the Visual Basic code of your macro, use the **Tools, Macro, Visual Basic Editor** command. If the macro is not in memory a blank Visual Basic screen is displayed in which case you will have to use the **Tools, Macro** command from the Visual Basic menu bar, specify which macro you want to edit by highlighting it, and pressing the **Edit** button. If the macro is in memory, actioning the editor automatically displays the memory's contents, as shown below.

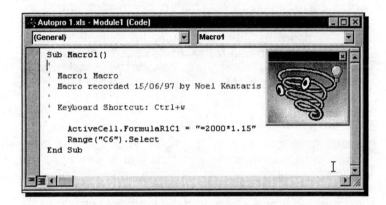

Before executing this macro, activate worksheet **Project 3** and change the entry in cell B6 back to its original value of 2000 (it was changed by 15% while you were typing the latest macro commands), then save the macros with the worksheet, but giving your workbook the filename **Autopro 1**. This is a simple precaution because, should things go wrong and your macro does unpredictable things to your worksheet, it will be easier to reopen the original worksheet than it would be to correct it!

To run the first macro, place the cell pointer on cell B6, then press **Ctrl+w**. The shortcut key starts the macro and changes automatically the entry in B6 by 15%.

133

Programming Advantages with Visual Basic

When the macros you write become more complicated, there are many advantages in using Visual Basic rather than using a macro command language that earlier versions of Excel and other spreadsheet packages used.

In Visual Basic you can assign values directly to variables instead of storing a value in a name as you would have to do in the macro command language. Variables can be made available to all procedures, to just the procedure in a module, or to just a single procedure, thus being far more flexible than names. In addition, in Visual Basic you can define constants to hold static values that you refer to repeatedly.

Reading Visual Basic Code:

Referring to our simple example, you can see that Visual Basic has created a macro that is preceded by comment statements (that start with an apostrophe (')) in which you are informed of the name of the macro, who created it and when, and the keyboard shortcut.

The macro commands are placed in between the two keywords **Sub** and **End Sub** which mark the beginning and end of a macro. In general, keywords, variables, operators, and procedure calls are referred to as statements which are the instructions to Excel to perform some action.

The statement

```
ActiveCell.FormulaR1C1 = "=2000*1.15"
```

is the way that Visual Basic enters the formula **=2000*1.15** into the active cell. In Visual Basic terminology; it uses the **Range** object to identify the range you want to change and sets the **Formula** property of the range to assign a formula to the range.

An 'object' is something you control in Visual Basic. Each object has characteristics called 'properties' which control the appearance of the object. Objects also have 'methods' which are actions that they can take.

In Visual Basic, you use:

- Objects (such as Workbooks, Worksheets, Ranges, Charts) to perform a task. Each object has characteristics, called properties, that make that object useful by controlling the appearance or behaviour of an object.

- Properties (such as ActiveCell, ActiveSheet, Value, Selection, ColumnWidth, RowHeight), to examine the condition of an object by returning the value of one of the object's properties (such as a character string for Value, a numeric value for ColumnWidth, True, or False).

- Methods which are actions that objects can do (such as Calculate, Clear, Copy, Justify, or Table). Methods are a part of objects just like properties. The difference between them is that properties have values which are set or returned, while methods are actions you would like an object to perform.

Should you want to learn to program in Visual Basic, then may we suggest you start with the book *Programming in Visual Basic for Windows* (BP346), also published by BERNARD BABANI (publishing) Ltd.

Editing a Macro

A macro can be edited by opening the file that contains it, and using the **Tools, Macro, Visual Basic Editor** command to load the Visual Basic editor, selecting the macro, and pressing the **Edit** button on the displayed dialogue box, as discussed earlier.

Since each of the three months in our worksheet is to be changed, we can edit all Macro1 references to Macro2, copy the highlighted entries and paste them twice before the **End Sub** statement. Next, change these appropriately so that reference is made to the correct amount of wages in the **ActiveCell.Formula** command and the correct cell reference in the **Range().Select** command, as shown below.

Save this workbook under the filename **Autopro 2** before attempting to run the changed macro. Doing so, also saves Macro2 (which replaces Macro1). If your macro is correct, activating cell B6 and pressing **Ctrl+w** runs it and changes the values of the wages entries for the three months to those shown on the worksheet window on the previous page.

We could use the same macro to find out the effect of increasing wages by different percentages by editing it, but this would be rather inefficient. A better method is to allocate a cell for the % increase, say cell G5, and edit the macro so that reference to that cell is made in the R1C1 absolute format. In this example, from cell B6 we would have to refer to R[-1]C[5] (Row 1 above present position, Column 5 from present position) which is the reference to cell G5 from B6.

Edit Macro2 to Macro3 and save the worksheet as **Autopro 3**.

Macro Interaction with Keyboard:

A further addition to the above macros could be made to allow for user entry of the 'increment' value from the keyboard, rather than having to edit cell G5. This can be achieved by using **InputBox()** macro command, which creates a dialogue box, as shown below, and returns the information entered into it.

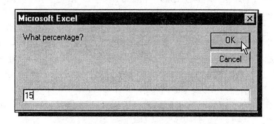

The general format of this macro command is:

```
Variable = InputBox("message")
```

and returns the value typed on the keyboard into the *variable*.

In the macro shown on the next page, we have tried to show the power of Visual Basic without making the example too complicated. First you are asked to give a percentage rate, then the macro calculates the increment and places the value of rate in G5, and stores the original contents of B6:D6 into the three variables, Xjan, Xfeb, and Xmar.

Next, the calculations take place and the results are entered in cell range B6:D6. Finally, a dialogue box is displayed (it can be moved out of the way) asking you to press the **OK** button in order to restore the original contents to the 'Wages' cell range, and changes the contents of G5 to 0 (zero).

Note: This macro only works if the active worksheet is **Sheet1** when you start the macro. If the active sheet is the macro module, then a run time error is encountered.

Finally, save this workbook as **Autopro 4** before attempting to run it.

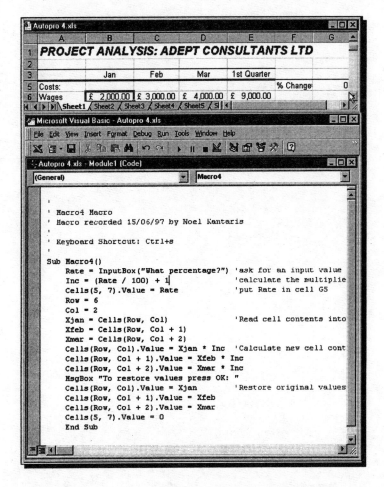

To start the macro, activate cell B6 and press **Ctrl+s**.

Visual Basic has many more statements, commands and functions which can be used to build and run your application in special ways. What we have tried to do here is to introduce you to the subject and give you some idea of the power of this programming language. A fuller explanation of Visual Basic is beyond the scope of this book.

9. EXERCISES USING EXCEL 97

The following exercises will help you to get going on your own and might be of interest to you. We give you as much guidance as we think is needed for you to complete them by yourself. Good luck

Compound Interest

To illustrate the behaviour of interest rates, set up an Excel 97 worksheet, as shown below, to calculate the compound interest of money lent over a certain period of time. Plot the resultant yearly interest against time, on the same graph, for three different values of interest rates.

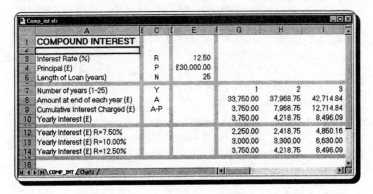

Compound interest is calculated using the formula

$$A = P * (1+R/100)^Y$$

where P is the principal (original money) lent, and A is what it amounts to in time Y years at an interest rate R% per annum. The cumulative interest charged is A-P.

Carry out the calculation on a yearly basis to the full period of the loan (N=25) years, with a constant value of Principal (P=£30,000), but with variable values of interest rate R, namely 7.5, 10 and 12.5%.

Type in your formulae in the worksheet in such a way (by making absolute reference to cells E3 to E5) as to allow you to copy these in the rows below the 'number of years' range that stretches from column G to column AE. You should then only need to change the value of R for the required 'Yearly Interest' to be calculated automatically in row 10.

The **Edit, Fill, Series** command can be used to fill the 'Number of Years' range with incremental data, while the **Edit, Copy** and **Edit, Paste Special, Values** commands can be used to copy the values of 'Yearly Interest' for each value of R to the bottom of the sheet for subsequent graphing. Copying by value is necessary to avoid changes to the data when R is changed.

Format your worksheet as shown on the previous page (or better), and use the information in cells A12:A14 plus G12:EA14, by first highlighting the first cell block, then pressing the <Ctrl> key down and while keeping it depressed, highlighting the second cell block. Next, action the Chart Wizard, select the chart of your choice and specify Sheet2 as the placement area.

Note that you might have to change the font size of the title, axes labels, and legends, and also re-size the chart to get what is shown below.

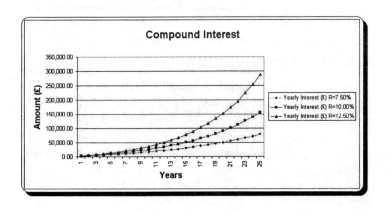

Product Sales Calculations

The first column shown below holds the 'part numbers' which identify a product, while the second and third columns hold the 'cost price' and '% profit' required from the sale of each product. The fourth column holds information on the 'Number of items sold', as follows:

Part No.	Cost Price (£)	% Profit	No. Sold
127	5.6	110	2500
130	6.5	130	1300
133	7	115	2800
136	6.25	125	1900
139	7.25	118	2300
142	7.5	135	2550
145	6.75	120	1800
148	6	133	3200
151	6.55	128	2750
154	7.55	122	1750
157	5.95	119	1950
160	6.16	124	2850

Assuming that the VAT rate is 17.5%, but can be changed subsequently to some other value, use Excel to calculate the following, assuming the relationships given on the next page:

(a) the sale price for each part,
(b) the VAT charged/unit,
(c) the total income,
(c) the sales cost, and
(d) the profit made.

Use the layout shown below for the input data, and the calculated results. You will need to enter the following relationships in columns I to M, respectively:

Column I:
Sale price_unit=Cost price_unit*(I+% profit_unit/100)*(I+VAT%/100)
Column J:
VAT charged_unit=Cost price_unit*(I+% profit_unit/100)*(VAT%/100)
Column K:
Total income=Sale price_unit * No. sold
Column L:
Total sales cost=(Cost price_unit+VAT charged_unit)*No. sold
Column M:
Profit made=(Sale price_unit*No. sold)–Total sales cost.

Format your worksheet as shown below (or better), and make provision for displaying the 'Total Profit made' and 'Total VAT charged' to also be displayed in cells C8 and C9 respectively.

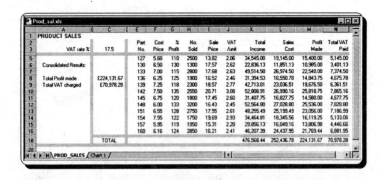

Having done so, then define a graph to plot Product Part No. versus the profit made for each product and the corresponding volume of sales of each product. Annotate, title and save your graph within the workbook, but on a different sheet than that used for the calculations.

Salary Calculations

A firm employs several persons who are identified by a unique 'works number' only, as shown in the sample table below. The first column of the table holds the 'works number' which identifies a person, while the second column holds the 'annual salary' (in £) of that person. The third and fourth columns of the table hold information relating to the 'overtime' worked (in hours) per month, and the corresponding 'hourly rate' (in £), respectively.

Employee Works No.	Annual Income	Overtime (hrs/month)	Overtime rate (£/hr)
93001	18850	14	14
93002	48500	10	29
93003	69750	6	40
93004	12900	18	16
93005	24350	6	17

The company would like to hold on record, not only the above information for each employee, but also information on the

    Monthly Overtime Income,
    Total Monthly N.I.,
    Monthly Tax on Gross Yearly Income,
    Monthly Tax on Overtime,
    Total Monthly Income, and
    Total Monthly Tax.

We propose to use an Excel worksheet to calculate and hold this information, but for simplicity we will assume that a person pays 11% of their monthly gross salary (excluding overtime) towards N.I. (National Insurance), while what is left is taxed at 25%. In addition, all earnings on overtime are taxed at 40%.

Use the layout suggested below to carry out these calculations. Devise your own formulae for the required calculations. Type in your formulae in the worksheet in such a way (by making absolute reference to cells C2 to C4) as to allow you to copy these easily. You should then only need to change the values of tax rates and/or N.I., for the information in the consolidated area of the worksheet (C9 to C11) to be calculated automatically.

Use the following input values:

Tax Rate X = 25%,
Tax Rate Y = 40%, and
National Insurance = 11%.

Format your worksheet as shown below (or better).

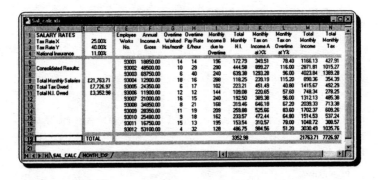

Having achieved the above, then define a stacked bar chart to plot the Total Monthly Income, Total Monthly Tax, and Total Monthly N.I. versus Employee Works No. Annotate, title and save your chart within the workbook, but on a different sheet.

10. FUNCTIONS

Excel's functions are built-in formulae that perform specialised calculations. Their general format is:

name(arg1,arg2,...)

where 'name' is the function name, and 'arg1', 'arg2', etc., are the arguments required for the evaluation of the function. Arguments must appear in a parenthesized list as shown above and their exact number depends on the function being used. However, some functions do not require arguments and are used without parentheses. Examples of these are: FALSE, NA, NOW, PI, RAND, TODAY and TRUE.

There are four types of arguments used with functions: numeric values, range values, string values and conditions, the type used being dependent on the type of function. Numeric value arguments can be entered either directly as numbers, as a cell address, a cell range name or as a formula. Range value arguments can be entered either as a range address or a range name, while string value arguments can be entered as an actual value (a string in double quotes), as a cell address, a cell name, or a formula. Condition arguments normally use logical operators or refer to an address containing a logic formula.

Types of Functions

There are several types of functions in Excel 97, namely, financial, date and time, mathematical and trigonometric, statistical, lookup and reference, database, text, logical, and information. Each type of function requires its own number and type of arguments. These are listed on the next few pages under the various function categories. To find out in detail how these functions can be used, click the Edit Formula button (■) to display:

147

Clicking the down-arrow to the left of the formula bar reveals the most recently used functions. Selecting the last item on the list will display the Paste Function dialogue box which lists all the available functions. Next, choose a function from the displayed list, and activate the Assistant from within this dialogue box. The characteristic yellow banner of the Assistant appears, as shown below, on which you can select to get 'Help with this feature'.

The Assistant then invokes the Excel 97 Help system which displays a whole page of information on each selected function, with examples on how to use it. In what follows, we list all the functions and what they return in a concise form for ease of selection, and so that you can see at a glance what is available .

Financial Functions:

Financial functions evaluate loans, annuities, depreciation and cash flows over a period of time, using numeric arguments. Where an optional parameter [Tp] is given the function will calculate for either an ordinary annuity or an annuity due, depending on the value you specified for type Tp. Percentages should be entered either as a decimal (for example, 0.155) or with a percent sign (for example, 15.5%). The various functions and what they return are as follows:

Function	Returns
DB(Ct,Sg,Lf,Pd)	The depreciation allowance of an asset with an initial value of Ct, life Lf, a final salvage value Sg for a specified period Pd, using the **declining balance** method.
DDB(Ct,Sg,Lf,Pd)	The **double-declining** depreciation allowance of an asset, with original cost Ct, predicted salvage value Sg, life Lf, and period Pd.
FV(Rt,Tm,Pt)	The **future value** of a series of equal payments, each of equal amount Pt, earning a periodic interest rate Rt, over a number of payment periods in term Tm.
IPMT(Rt,Pr,Tm,Pv)	The **interest payment** for a given period Pr (which must be between 1 and Tm) of a total term Tm of a loan with present value Pv at a constant interest rate Rt.
IRR(Rg,Gs)	The **internal rate of return** of range Rg of cash flows, based on the approximate percentage guess Gs.

MIRR(Rg,Fr,Rr)	The **modified internal rate of return** for a series of cashflows in a range Rg, with interest rates Fr, paid on money used in cash flows and Rr received on reinvested cash flows.
NPER(Rt,Pt,Pv,Fv)	The **number of periods** required for a series of equal payments Pt, with a present-value Pv, to accumulate a future-value Fv, at a periodic interest rate Rt.
NPV(Rt,Rg)	The **net present value** of the series of future cash flows in range Rg, discounted at a periodic interest rate Rt.
PMT(Rt,Tm,Pv,Fv)	The **payment** on a loan with present value Pv, at interest rate Rt, for Tm number of payments and future value Fv.
PPMT(Rt,Pr,Tm,Pv,Fv)	The **principal portion** of the periodic payment on a loan of present value Pv, at interest rate Rt, for payment periods Pr (the number of payment periods in an annuity), leading to a future value Fv.
PV(Rt,Tm,Pt)	The **present value** of a series of payments, each of amount Pt, discounted at a periodic interest rate Rt, over a number of payment periods in term Tm.
RATE(Tm,Pt,Pv,Fv)	The **periodic interest rate** necessary for a present value Pv to grow to a future value Fv, over the number of compounding periods in term Tm at Pt payments per period.

SLN(Ct,Sg,Lf)	The **straight line depreciation** of an asset of cost Ct for one period, given its predicted salvage value Sg, and life Lf.
SYD(Ct,Sg,Lf,Pd)	The **sum-of-years' digits depreciation** of an asset of cost Ct, given its predicted salvage value Sg, life Lf, and period Pd.
VDB(Ct,Sg,Lf,S,E,*d,s*)	The **depreciation** of an asset of cost Ct, salvage value Sg, life Lf, over a period from start S to end E. Depreciation-factor *d* and switch *s,* are optional. If *s* is 1 it returns declining balance depreciation for life, else straight-line is used after E.

Date and Time Functions:

These generate and use serial numbers with dates having integer serial numbers between 1 and 65380 to represent dates between 1 January, 1900 and 31 December 2078, and time having decimal serial numbers starting with 0.000 at midnight and ending with 0.99999 next midnight. The various functions are:

Function	*Returns*
DATE(Yr,Mh,Dy)	The date number of argument Yr,Mh,Dy.
DATEVALUE(Ts)	The number of days from 1 January 1900 of date string Ts.
DAY(Dn)	The day of the month number (1-31) of date number Dn.
DAYS360(Sn,En)	The number of days between Sn and En, based on a year of 12 months, each of 30 days.
HOUR(Tn)	The hour number (0-23) of time number Tn.

151

MINUTE(Tn)	The minute number (0-59) of time number Tn.
MONTH(Dn)	The month number (1-12) of date number Dn.
NOW()	The serial number for the current date and time.
SECOND(Tn)	The second number (0-59) of time number Tn.
TIME(Hr,Ms,Ss)	The time number of argument Hr,Ms,Ss.
TIMEVALUE(Ts)	The time number of string Ts.
TODAY()	The current date number.
WEEKDAY(Dn)	The day of the week from date number Dn in integer form; 0 (Monday) through 6 (Sunday).
YEAR(Dn)	Returns the year number (0-199) of date number Dn.

Mathematical and Trigonometric Functions:

These functions evaluate a result using numeric arguments. The various functions and what they return are as follows:

Function	*Returns*
ABS(X)	The absolute value of X.
ACOS(X)	The angle in radians, whose cosine is X (arc cos of X).
ACOSH(N)	The arc (inverse) hyperbolic cosine of number N.
ASIN(X)	The angle in radians, whose sine is X (arc sin of X).
ASINH(N)	The arc (inverse) hyperbolic sine of number N.

ATAN(X)	The angle in radians, between $\pi/2$ and $-\pi/2$, whose tangent is X (arc tan of X - 2 quadrant).
ATAN2(X,Y)	The angle in radians, between π and $-\pi$, whose tangent is Y/X (arc tan of Y/X - 4 quadrant).
ATANH(N)	The arc (inverse) hyperbolic tangent of number N.
CEILING(N,Sig)	The rounded value of N to nearest integer or nearest multiple of significance Sig.
COMBIN(N,Obj)	The number of combinations N for a given number of objects Obj.
COS(X)	The cosine of X (X in radians).
COSH(X)	The hyperbolic cosine of X.
DEGREES(X)	The value in degrees of X radians.
EVEN(X)	The rounded value of X away from 0 to the nearest even integer.
EXP(X)	The value of e raised to the power of X.
FACT(X)	The factorial of X.
FLOOR(N, Sig)	A number N rounded down towards zero by nearest multiple of significance Sig.
INT(X)	The integer part of X.
LN(X)	The natural log (base e) of X.
LOG(X,N)	The log of X to a specified base N.
LOG10(X)	The log (base 10) of X.

MDETERM(Ar)	The matrix determinant of an array.
MINVERSE(Ar)	The matrix inverse of an array.
MMULT(Ar1,Ar2)	The matrix product of two arrays.
MOD(X,Y)	The remainder of X/Y.
ODD(X)	The rounded value of X away from 0 to the nearest odd integer.
PI()	The value of π (3.1415926).
POWER(X,N)	The value of X raised to the power of N.
PRODUCT(Ls)	The result of multiplying the values in list Ls.
RADIANS(X)	The value in radians of X degrees.
RAND()	A random number between 0 and 1.
ROMAN(N,Fm)	The Roman format Fm (as text) of number N.
ROUND(X,N)	The value of X rounded to N places.
ROUNDDOWN(X,N)	The rounded value of X down to the nearest multiple of the power of 10 specified by N.
ROUNDUP(X,N)	The rounded value of X up to the nearest multiple of the power of 10 specified by N.
SIGN(X)	The value of 1 if X is a positive, 0 if X is 0, and −1 if X is negative.
SIN(X)	The sine of angle X (X in rads).

SINH(X)	The hyperbolic sine of angle X (X in rads).
SQRT(X)	The square root of X.
SUBTOTAL(Ls)	The subtotal in a list Ls or a database.
SUM(Rg)	The sum of values in range Rg.
SUMIF(Rg,Cr)	The sum in range Rg that meet a given criteria Cr.
SUMPRODUCT(Ar1,Ar2)	The sum of the products of array components.
SUMSQ(N1,N2)	The sum of the squares of the arguments.
SUMX2MY2(Ar1,Ar2)	The sum of the difference of squares of corresponding values in two arrays.
SUMX2PY2(Ar1,Ar2)	The sum of the sum of squares of corresponding values in two arrays.
SUMXMY2(Ar1,Ar2)	The sum of squares of differences of corresponding values in two arrays.
TAN(X)	The tangent of angle X (X in rads).
TANH(X)	The hyperbolic tangent of angle X (X in rads).
TRUNC(X,N)	The truncated value of X to N decimal places.

Statistical Functions:

Statistical functions evaluate lists of values using numeric arguments or cell ranges. The various functions and what they return are as follows:

Function	*Returns*
AVEDEV(Ls)	The average of the absolute deviations of values in list Ls.
AVERAGE(Rg)	The average of values in range Rg.
AVERAGEA(Rg)	The average (arithmetic mean) of values in range Rg, including logical values and text - evaluating text and FALSE as 0, and TRUE as 1.
BETADIST(X,Al,Bt,A,B)	The cumulative beta probability density function.
BETAINV(Pb,Al,Bt,A,B)	The inverse of the cumulative beta probability function.
BINOMDIST(Sc,Tr,Pb,Tp)	The cumulative distribution function if Tp is TRUE, else the probability mass function, with Tr independent trials and Sc successes in trials and Pr probability of success per trial.
CHIDIST(X,Fr)	The chi-square distribution, evaluated at X and Fr degrees of freedom for the sample.
CHINV(X,Fr)	The inverse of the one-tailed probability of the chi-squared distribution.
CHITEST(Rg1,Rg2)	The chi-square test for independence on the data in range Rg1, or a chi-square test for goodness of fit on the data in ranges Rg1 and Rg2.

CONFIDENCE(Al,Sd,Sz)	The confidence interval for a population mean.
CORREL(Rg1,Rg2)	The correlation coefficient of values in ranges Rg1 and Rg2.
COUNT(Ls)	The number of values in a list.
COUNTA(Rg)	The number of non-blank values in a range Rg.
COUNTBLANK(Rg)	The number of blank cells within range Rg.
COUNTIF(Rg, Cr)	The number of non-blank cells within a range Rg.
COVAR(Rg1,Rg2)	The sample covariance of the values in ranges Rg1 and Rg2.
CRITBINOM(Tr,Pb,Al)	The largest integer for which the cumulative binomial distribution is less than or equal to Al, with Tr Bernoulli trials and a probability of success for a single Bernoulli trial Pb.
DEVSQ(Ls)	The sum of squared deviations of the values in list Ls, from their mean.
EXPONDIST(X,Lm,Ds)	The exponential distribution.
FDIST(X,Fr1,Fr2)	The F-distribution at value X with Fr1 and Fr2 degrees of freedom for the first and second samples.
FINV(Pb,Fr1,Fr2)	The inverse of the F probability distribution.
FISHER(X)	The Fisher transformation.
FISHERINV(Y)	The inverse of the Fisher transformation.
FORECAST(X,Yo,Xo)	The value along a linear trend.

FREQUENCY(Rg,Bin)	The frequency distribution as a vertical array Bin.
FTEST(Rg1,Rg2)	The associated probability of an F-test on data in ranges Rg1 and Rg2. Used to determine if two samples have different variances.
GAMMADIST(X,Al,Bt,Cm)	The gamma distribution.
GAMMAINV(Pb,Al,Bt)	The inverse of the gamma cumulative distribution.
GAMMALN(X)	The natural logarithm of the gamma function.
GEOMEAN(Ls)	Returns the geometric mean of the values in list Ls.
GROWTH(Yo,Xo,Xn,Ct)	The values along an exponential trend.
HARMEAN(Ls)	The harmonic mean of the values in list Ls.
HYPGEOMDIST(Ns,Ssiz,Pp,Psiz)	The hypergeometric distribution probability of a given number of successes Ns, given the sample size Ssiz, population success Pp and population size Psiz.
INTERCEPT(Yo,Xo)	The intercept of the linear regression line.
KURT(Rg)	The kurtosis of the values in range Rg.
LARGE(Arr,K)	The largest value in a data set.
LINEST(Yo,Xo,Ct,St)	The parameters of a linear trend.
LOGEST(Yo,Xo,Ct,St)	The parameters of an exponential trend.

LOGINV(Pb,Mn,Sd)	The inverse of the lognormal distribution with parameters mean Mn and standard deviation Sd.
LOGNORMDIST(X,Mn,Sd)	
	The cumulative lognormal distribution with parameters mean Mn and standard deviation Sd.
MAX(Rg)	The maximum value in a range.
MAXA(Rg)	The maximum value in a range. Does not ignore logical values or text.
MEDIAN(Ls)	The median value in list Ls.
MIN(Rg)	The minimum value in a range.
MINA(Rg)	The minimum value in a range. Does not ignore logical values or text.
MODE(Ls)	The most common value in a data set.
NEGBINOMDIST(Nf,Ns,Pb)	
	The negative binomial distribution that there will be a number of failures Nf before the number of successes Ns, when the constant probability of success is Pb.
NORMDIST(X,Mn,Sd)	The normal cumulative distribution function for X, with a distribution mean Mn and optional standard deviation Sd.
NORMINV(Pb,Mn,Sd)	The inverse of the normal cumulative distribution.
NORMSDIST(X)	The standard normal cumulative distribution.

NORMSINV(Pb)	The inverse of the standard normal cumulative distribution.
PEARSON(Ar1,Ar2)	The Pearson product moment correlation coefficient.
PERCENTILE(Rg,K)	The Kth sample percentile among the values in range Rg.
PERCENTRANK(Ar,X,Sg)	The percentage rank of a value in a data set.
PERMUT(N,Nc)	The number of ordered sequences (permutations) of Nc chosen objects that can be selected from a total of N objects.
POISSON(X,Mn,Cm)	The Poisson distribution (depending on cumulative factor Cm) of X observed events and Mn expected number of events.
PROB(Rgx,Pb,Ll,Ul)	The probability that values in Rgx range are within lower limit Ll and upper limit Ul of probability Pb.
QUARTILE(Ar,Qrt)	The quartile of a data set.
RANK(It,Rg,Od)	The relative size or position of a value It in a range Rg, relative to other values in the range, ranked in order Od.
RSQ(Yo,Xo)	The square of the Pearson product moment correlation coefficient.
SKEW(Rg)	The skewness of the values in range Rg.
SLOPE(Yo,Xo)	The slope of the linear regression line.
SMALL(Ar,K)	The Kth smallest value in a data set.

STANDARDIZE(X,Mn,Sd)	The normalised value of X from a distribution characterised by mean Mn and standard deviation Sd.
STDEV(Rg)	The population standard deviation of values in range Rg.
STDEVA(Rg)	An estimate of the standard deviation based on a sample, including logical values and text.
STDEVP(Rg)	The standard deviation based on the entire population.
STDEVPA(Rg)	The standard deviation based on the entire population, including logical values and text.
STEYX(Yo,Xo)	The standard error of the predicted y-value for each X in the regression.
TDIST(X,Fr,Tr)	The Student's t-distribution, evaluated at X and Fr degrees of freedom for the sample, with test direction Tr.
TINV(Pb,Fr)	The inverse of the Student's t-distribution.
TREND(Xo,Yo,Xn,Cn	The values along a linear trend.
TRIMMEAN(Ar,Pb)	The mean of the interior of a data set.
TTEST(Rg1,Rg2,Tl,Tp)	The probability associated with a Student's t-test.
VAR(Rg)	The sample variance of values in range Rg.
VARA(Rg)	An estimate of the variance based on a sample, including logical values and text.

Function	Returns
VARP(Rg)	The variance of values in range Rg based on entire population.
VARPA(Rg)	The variance of values in range Rg based on entire population, including logical values and text.
WEIBULL(X,Al,Bt,Cm)	The Weibull distribution.
ZTEST(Arr,X,Sg)	Returns the two-tailed P-value of a z-test.

Lookup and Reference Functions:

The group of function return values specified by a range reference or array reference. The various functions available and what they return are as follows:

Function	*Returns*
ADDRESS(Rn,Cn)	The cell address specified by row Rn and column Cn.
AREAS(Rf1,Rf2,..)	The number of areas in the list of references.
CHOOSE(K,V0,..,Vn)	The Kth value in the list V0,..,Vn.
COLUMN(Rf)	The column number of a reference.
COLUMNS(Rg)	The number of columns in the range Rg.
HLOOKUP(X,Ar,Rn)	The value of indicated cell by performing a horizontal array look-up by comparing the value X to each cell in the top index row in array Ar, then moves down the column in which a match is found by the specified row number Rn.

HYPERLINK(Loc,Fn)	A shortcut to a document on your hard disc, network server of the Internet at specified location and friendly name.
INDEX(Rg,Rn,Cn)	The value of the cell in range Rg at the intersection of row-offset Rn, and column-offset Cn.
INDIRECT(Rf)	The cell reference specified in reference Rf in A1-style.
LOOKUP(Lv,Vr,Rv)	The relative position of an item in an array that matches a specified value in a specified order.
MATCH(Lv,Ar,Mtc)	The relative position of an element in an array Ar that matches the specified value Mtc of a lookup value Lv.
OFFSET(Rf,Rn,C,Ht,Wh)	A reference of a specified height Ht and width Wh offset from another reference Rf by a specified number of rows Rn and columns Cn.
ROW(Rf)	The row number of a reference.
ROWS(Rg)	The number of rows in a range.
TRANSPOSE(Ar)	The transpose of an array.
VLOOKUP(X,Ar,Cn)	The value of indicated cell by performing a vertical table lookup by comparing the value X to each cell in the first index column, in array Ar, then moves across the row in which a match is found by the specified column number Cn.

Database Functions:

Database functions perform calculations on a database. The database, called the input range, consists of records, which include fields and field names, like Fd below. A criterion range must be set up to select the records from the database that each function uses. The various functions and what they return are as follows:

Function	*Returns*
DAVERAGE(Db,Fd,Cr)	The average of the values in the field Fd that meet the criteria Cr in a database Db.
DCOUNT(Db,Fd,Cr)	The number of non-blank cells in the field Fd that meet the criteria Cr in a database Db.
DCOUNTA(Db,Fd,Cr)	Counts nonblank cells from a specified database and criteria.
DGET(Db,Fd,Cr)	The single value in the field Fd that meet the criteria Cr in a database Db.
DMAX(Db,Fd,Cr)	The maximum value in the field Fd that meet the criteria Cr in a database Db.
DMIN(Db,Fd,Cr)	The minimum value in the field Fd that meet the criteria Cr in a database Db.
DPRODUCT(Db,Fd,Cr)	The result of the product of the values in the field Fd that meet the criteria Cr in a database Db.
DSTDEV(Db,Fd,Cr)	The standard deviation based on the values in the field Fd that meet the criteria Cr in a database Db.

DSTDEVP(Db,Fd,Cr)	The standard deviation based on the entire population of the values in the field Fd that meet the criteria Cr in a database Db.
DSUM(Db,Fd,Cr)	The sum of the values in the field Fd that meet the criteria Cr in a database Db.
DVAR(Db,Fd,Cr)	The estimated variance based on the values in the field Fd that meet the criteria Cr in a database Db.
DVARP(Db,Fd,Cr)	The variance based on the entire population of the values in the field Fd that meet the criteria Cr in a database Db.
GETPIVOTDATA(Pt,Nm)	Data stored within a named pivotal table.

Text Functions:

String functions operate on strings and produce numeric or string values dependent on the function.

Function	*Returns*
CHAR(X)	The character that corresponds to the code number X.
CLEAN(Sg)	The specified string Sg having removed all non-printable characters from it.
CODE(Sg)	The code number for the first character in string Sg.
CONCATENATE(Sg1,Sg2)	
	One string made up of several strings.
DOLLAR(N,Dm)	A number in text form, using currency format.

EXACT(Sg1,Sg2)	The value 1 (TRUE) if strings Sg1 and Sg2 are exactly alike, otherwise 0 (FALSE).
FIND(Ss,Sg,Sn)	The position at which the first occurrence of search string Ss begins in string Sg, starting the search from search number Sn.
FIXED(N,Dm,Nc)	A number N formatted as text with a fixed number of decimals Dm. Nc is a logical value and if TRUE prevents the inclusion of commas.
LEFT(Sg,N)	The first (leftmost) N characters in string Sg.
LEN(Sg)	The number of characters in string Sg.
LOWER(Sg)	A string Sg with all the letters converted to lowercase.
MID(Sg,Sn,N)	The N characters from string Sg beginning with the character at Sn.
PROPER(Sg)	A string with all words in string Sg changed to first letter in uppercase and the rest in lowercase.
REPLACE(O,S,N,Ns)	A string with N characters removed from original string O, starting at character S and then inserts new string Ns in the vacated place.
REPT(Sg,N)	A repeated string Sg, N times. Unlike the repeating character (\), the output is not limited by the column width.

RIGHT(Sg,N)	The last (rightmost) N characters in string Sg.
SEARCH(Sg1,O,S)	String Sg1 in original string O, starting at character S.
SUBSTITUTE(Sg,O,Ns,N)	A new string Ns substituted for old string O in a string Sg. N specifies which occurrence of the old text you want to replace.
T(X)	A value X converted into text.
TEXT(X,Fm)	A number X formatted into text.
TRIM(Sg)	A string Sg with no leading, trailing or consecutive spaces.
UPPER(Sg)	All letters in string Sg converted to uppercase.
VALUE(Sg)	The numeric value of string Sg.

Logical Functions:

Logical functions produce a value based on the result of a conditional statement, using numeric arguments. The various functions and what they return are as follows:

Function	*Returns*
AND(N1,N2,N3,..)	The logical value 1 (TRUE) if all its arguments are TRUE.
FALSE()	The logical value 0.
IF(Cr,X,Y)	The value X if Cr is TRUE and Y if Cr is FALSE.
NOT(N)	The reverse logic of its argument N.
OR(N1, N2, ..)	The logical value 1 (TRUE) if any argument is TRUE.
TRUE()	The logical value 1.

Information Functions:

Information functions perform a variety of advanced tasks, such as looking up values in a table, returning information about cells, ranges or the Excel environment. The various functions and what they return are as follows:

Function	*Returns*
CELL(At,Rg)	Returns the code representing the attribute At of range Rg.
ERROR.TYPE(X)	The error value.
INFO(At)	Returns system information based on the attribute At.
ISBLANK(X)	The value 1 (TRUE), if X is an empty cell.
ISERR(X)	1 (TRUE), if X is an error value except #N/A.
ISERROR(X)	1 (TRUE), if X is any error.
ISLOGICAL(X)	1 (TRUE), if X is a logical value.
ISNA(X)	1 (TRUE), if X contains #N/A.
ISNONTEXT(X)	1 (TRUE), if X is not text.
ISNUMBER(X)	1 (TRUE), if X contains a numeric value.
ISREF(X)	1(TRUE), if X is a reference.
ISTEXT(X)	1 (TRUE), if X is text.
N(X)	A value converted to a number
NA()	The error value #N/A.
TYPE(X)	A number indicating the data type value of X.

INDEX

COMPANION DISCS TO BOOKS

COMPANION DISCS are available for most books written by the same author(s) and published by BERNARD BABANI (publishing) LTD, as listed at the front of this book (except for those marked with an asterisk). These books contain many pages of file/program listings. There is no reason why you should spend hours typing them into your computer, unless you wish to do so, or need the practice.

COMPANION DISCS come in 3½" format with all example listings.

ORDERING INSTRUCTIONS

To obtain your copy of a companion disc, fill in the order form below or a copy of it, enclose a cheque (payable to **P.R.M. Oliver**) or a postal order, and send it to the address below. Make sure you fill in your name and address and specify the book number and title in your order.

Book No.	Book Name	Unit Price	Total Price
BP		£3.50	
BP		£3.50	
BP		£3.50	
Name		Sub-total	£.............
Address:		P & P (@ 45p/disc)	£.............
		Total Due	£.............

Send to: P.R.M. Oliver, CSM, Pool, Redruth, Cornwall, TR15 3SE

PLEASE NOTE
The author(s) are fully responsible for providing this Companion Disc service. The publishers of this book accept no responsibility for the supply, quality, or magnetic contents of the disc, or in respect of any damage, or injury that might be suffered or caused by its use.